THE NEW TESTAMENT AND JEWISH LAW:
A GUIDE FOR THE PERPLEXED

THE NEW TESTAMENT AND JEWISH LAW: A GUIDE FOR THE PERPLEXED

JAMES G. CROSSLEY

t&t clark

Published by T&T Clark International
A Continuum Imprint
The Tower Building, 11 York Road, London SE1 7NX
80 Maiden Lane, Suite 704, New York, NY 10038

www.continuumbooks.com

British Library Cataloguing-in-Publication Data
A catalogue record for this book is available from the British Library.

ISBN: 978-0-567-03433-5 (Hardback)
978-0-567-03434-2 (Paperback)

Library of Congress Cataloging-in-Publication Data
A catalog record for this book is available from the Library of Congress.

Typeset by Newgen Imaging Systems Pvt Ltd, Chennai, India
Printed and bound in Great Britain by CPI Antony Rowe Ltd,
Chippenham, Wiltshire

For Maurice Casey

CONTENTS

ACKNOWLEDGEMENTS

I would like, as ever, to thank Francis Crossley, Pamela Crossley, Richard Crossley, Gill Turner, Caroline Watt, Glennis Watt, and Mike Watt. But I have to single out the perfect duo: Serena and Dominique Crossley.

I would like to thank Haaris Naqvi and Dominic Mattos for supporting this book and being nice when things got too busy.

I have been writing about and teaching on Jewish Law for over ten years. This was initially due to the inspiration of Maurice Casey who, in a scholarly world full of people not prepared to read the details of Jewish Law in their original languages, has shown himself to be a righteous Gentile indeed!

INTRODUCTION

In the history of New Testament scholarship, and Christianity more generally, Jewish Law has had a bad press. Right up to the 1970s, the dominant view of Jewish Law in relation to the New Testament was that those dedicated to its practices represented a religion (Judaism) which was cold, harsh, legalistic and, of course, a negative backdrop for the new religion of grace, Christianity, effectively represented by figures such as Jesus and Paul. This was all part of a general cultural context whereby Judaism was seen as an inferior religion to Christianity and where Jews were seen as a particular problem for social categorization. These views reached their infamous low point in Nazi Germany and the Holocaust.

General attitudes did not start to change among New Testament scholars in any serious sense until the 1970s, particularly with the publication of E. P. Sanders' *Paul and Palestinian Judaism* (1977). Sanders challenged the dominant negative view of Jewish Law and Judaism as a cold, harsh religion, obsessed with earning salvation through observance of the commandments. Instead, Sanders argued, the general pattern of Jewish religion was to be labelled 'covenantal nomism'. This involved 'getting in', that is God making a covenant with Israel after the graceful election of Israel, and 'staying in', that is Israel maintaining this relationship by obeying the commandments. Within this system, God remained merciful to Israel and provided means of atoning for sin. Sanders has since gone on to write a technical book on Jewish Law around the time of Christian origins, *Jewish*

Law from Jesus to the Mishnah (1990), a landmark publication in the study of Jewish Law in relationship to the New Testament. Along with the work of scholars such as Bernard Jackson, Geza Vermes, Jacob Neusner, Markus Bockmuehl and David Instone-Brewer (to name a few), there is a lot of detailed study of Jewish Law which is theoretically available to New Testament scholars. Much of this work is, however, highly technical and one of the aims of this book is to provide a more simplified introduction to Jewish Law for New Testament studies.

Yet, despite the best efforts of scholars such as those named above, the specifics of Jewish Law are still regularly misunderstood in New Testament studies.[1] Even ideas surrounding 'covenantal nomism', important though they undoubtedly are, are understood in terms of systematic *Christian* theology, such as the language of grace and works. This is not the place to get involved with Christian theology and issues of works versus grace but I think it is worth stressing that this sort of debate still often works with the assumption that works are somehow *wrong, theologically wrong*, or even *morally wrong* because frequently the idea is that Judaism must have a strong concept of God's grace and less emphasis on human works. But if it so happened that masses of ancient Jewish sources were found which conclusively showed that much of Judaism really did believe that works were the way to salvation, what would we do then? This book will work with the assumption that people concerned, even obsessed, with details of the Law are neither wrong nor right and it will leave the theological issues of grace and salvation to theologians that way inclined. By looking at the details of Jewish Law I am not intending that this book supports the view that Jews were obsessed with details of the Law or the view that plenty of Jews were not. It is certainly possible to make a reasonable case that the author of this book is obsessed with Jewish Law (a claim that has actually been made) and this author probably would not disagree.

One reason why I am suspicious of some of the judgements made on Jewish Law is that that those praising Jewish Law conceal theological agendas just as those earlier judgements of scholars from a previous generation (e.g. Rudolf Bultmann) did. The work of N. T. Wright on Jesus is flawed for many reasons but one of them is his handling of Jewish Law. Wright is full of high praise for Jewish Law. Yet it is one thing to repeatedly praise how wonderful the Law was but this rings a little hollow when he repeatedly ignores the details of Jewish Law when he discusses Jesus' attitude towards the Law. For instance, on the issue of family and ethnicity, Wright emphasizes that Jewish texts such as Ezra 10 may sound extreme to us but were fairly tame by ancient standards and were part of the self-preservation of the Jewish people. This is not, as Wright points out in his defence of Judaism, 'in any way discreditable (however often people have thought so)'. But after pointing out the positives, Wright then says that Jesus, 'to put it mildly, set a time-bomb beside this symbol . . . and realized that some of the symbols had now become (not wicked, or shoddy, but) redundant'. On texts such as Mt. 8.21–22/Lk. 9.59–60, Wright argues that Jesus' comments are 'quite frankly, outrageous . . . astonishing'. But then Wright qualifies such statements to make sure Judaism does not come out too badly: 'we must stress that this does not mean that Jesus thought such a symbol inherently bad, or even second rate . . . '[2] Wright's view of family and ethnicity may be based on fair generalizations but he focuses on the details of the New Testament texts while avoiding the details of *Jewish* texts. This allows him to make the argument that the sayings attributed to Jesus are, apparently, shocking. But what if Jesus' sayings were sentiments paralleled in Jewish Law and early Judaism? And is not Wright simply perpetuating the old idea of Judaism as a backdrop to make Christianity better? *Details* are, then, important.

But I do not want this introductory book to be polemical. What I want to do is to introduce Jewish legal sources which have obvious thematic relevance for the study of the New Testament, in addition to being prominent in early Jewish sources outside the New Testament. The topics chosen reflect this: Sabbath; purity and food; divorce, 'eye for an eye', oaths and vows; and ethnicity and interaction with Gentiles.

This book will also provide extensive quotations from Jewish sources. My experience of teaching Jewish Law, and early Judaism in general, is that these sources are quite alien to students and some of the topics, especially purity, are particularly complex. The use of primary sources will hopefully illuminate those topics and explanations which may be alien and complex to many readers.

There will be little in the way of detailed exegesis of New Testament texts in this book. While a gentle exegetical prodding cannot always be avoided, one of the main aims of this book is to provide texts and themes which can then be used by readers to interpret New Testament texts. Some of these texts and themes may or may not be of the right chronological time and geographical place but in many cases these texts are the closest parallels we have. I leave it up to readers to follow up and decide how relevant some of the later texts may be.

But before we look at specific legal texts, it is worth outlining the ways in which Jewish Law was understood and interpreted in early Judaism.

CHAPTER 1

INTERPRETING JEWISH LAW
IN EARLY JUDAISM

From the outset it must be strongly emphasized that the following short history and analysis of Jewish interpretation of the Law is very basic and only a general outline. Much, much more can be written and so what will be done here is to cover some of the key issues which will be of relevance for the rest of this book. I will cover a period close to one millennium, from the final form of the biblical texts through to rabbinic literature. The major focus will be on the different ways in which the Law was interpreted by different Jewish groups, but some space will be devoted to the role of the Law as a whole in Jewish identity and reactions against, as well as interactions with, different cultural contexts. With these explicit qualifications in mind, we can turn to the earliest interpreters of the Law.

THE LAW AND ITS EARLIEST INTERPRETERS

In very basic terms we can say that the Law or Torah is simply the first five books of the Bible, namely, Genesis, Exodus, Numbers, Leviticus and Deuteronomy, otherwise known collectively as the Pentateuch. What we can probably say with a reasonable degree of certainty is that the Pentateuch was brought together in more or less the final form we have it in the Persian period (538–332 BCE), in the aftermath of the exilic period (587/586 BCE–538/537 BCE) when the first Temple was destroyed, certain Judeans were exiled, and those 'exiled' in Babylon returned. Echoes of related themes may be seen throughout the Pentateuch (cf. Gen. 6.5–8; 11; Exod. 2.23–24; 3.16–22; 16–7; 20.5; Num. 24.8, 23; Deut. 5.9; 6.10–12; 7.10; 29.17–29). The Pentateuch contains many, if not most, practices which became associated with Jewish behaviour in the ancient world, such as the avoidance of eating pork, avoidance of working on the Sabbath, a range of ethical teaching, purity laws and so on.

Not even the lengthy legal sections of the Pentateuch could deal with all of the issues raised in daily life and nor could they deal with changing historical and social circumstances. Some biblical laws needed re-interpreting in light of new circumstances. It is one thing to avoid work on the Sabbath but then what constitutes 'work'? Plucking grain and eating it (cf. Mk 2.23–28; Mt. 12.1–8; Lk. 6.1–6)? Here it might be worth thinking of this issue in a two-fold manner: (1) biblical Law, i.e. the laws as stated in the Hebrew Bible/Old Testament; and (2) the interpretation or expansion of biblical Law, i.e. interpreting the biblical laws to fit new situations, sometimes called 'tradition' or 'tradition of the elders' in ancient sources. It should be emphasized from the outset that this two-fold distinction is not hard-and-fast. Some interpreters of biblical laws believed that their interpretation was implicit in the biblical Law or that Moses was as much linked in with the interpretation as he was with, for example, the Ten Commandments.

This two-fold distinction will be used to highlight different interpretations by different groups and as a means of comparison (we will see that certain ancient sources compared with something like this two-fold distinction). It is clear, after all, that plenty of people agreed with the principle of, for instance, Sabbath observance but disagreed with how 'work' should be interpreted (see Chapter 2). By the time of the New Testament the detailed interpretation and re-interpretation of biblical Law had a long history. We may begin with two books which came to be closely associated with one another, namely Ezra and Nehemiah.

The books of Ezra and Nehemiah tell the story of the return of the exiles under Persian rule. Quite when Ezra and Nehemiah were written is not clear but, for our present purposes, precision is not important. All we need claim for now is that scholars have argued that they were written down, in something like their final form, in either the Persian period (538–332 BCE) or early in the Hellenistic period (332–63 BCE), and so were written, obviously, centuries prior to the New Testament. This point is important because it seems as if at least some parts of biblical Law, if not all of biblical Law as a coherent and collected whole (cf. Ezra 7), were available to the writers of Ezra and Nehemiah because in these books we find examples of re-interpretation and re-application of certain biblical verses as Hugh Williamson in has shown in a still impressive piece of exegesis.[1]

One of the more prominent examples of such early biblical interpretation concerns mixed marriages in Ezra 9.1–2:

> After these things had been done, the officials approached me and said, 'The people of Israel, the priests, and the Levites have not separated themselves from the peoples of the lands with their abominations, from the Canaanites, the Hittites, the Perizzites, the Jebusites, the Ammonites, the Moabites, the Egyptians, and the Amorites. For they have taken some of their daughters as wives for themselves and for their sons. Thus the holy seed has mixed itself with the peoples of the lands, and in this faithlessness the officials and leaders have led the way'.

Despite plenty of stories about foreign marital partners in the Bible (e.g. Gen. 16.3; 41.45; Exod. 2.21; Num. 12.1; 2 Sam. 3.3), it is clear that sentiments similar to Ezra 9.1–2 are found in the Pentateuch (e.g. Exod. 34.11–16; Deut. 20.10–18), especially Deut. 7.1–4 which seems to be a basis for Ezra 9.1–2. Even so, the list of peoples in Ezra 9.1–2 appears to be an example of bringing together three different biblical verses dealing with related issues. Reference to the Hittites, the Amorites, the Canaanites, the Perizzites and the Jebusites can be found in Deut. 7.1, the Ammonites and the Moabites can be found Deut. 23.3, and the Egyptians may be a reference to the discussion of forbidden marriages in Leviticus 18, and with Lev. 18.3 more precisely in mind, 'You shall not do as they do in the land of Egypt, where you lived, and you shall not do as they do in the land of Canaan, to which I am bringing you. You shall not follow their statutes'.

In the passages from the Pentateuch, the problem with mixed marriages primarily concerned idolatry. For instance, in Ezra 9.2 there is clearly a reference to Deut. 7.3, 'you shall not intermarry with them [the Hittites, the Girgashites etc.], giving your daughters to their sons or taking their daughters for your sons, for that would turn away your children from following me, to serve other gods'. But Ezra 9.1–2 takes this one step further when it gives the justification that 'the holy seed has mixed itself with the peoples of the lands'. Here we see the text moving towards a hard ethnic differentiation. While the language of 'seed' has some background in the promises to Abram/Abraham but in Genesis 12 (e.g. Gen. 12.1–3, 7), there is the idea of bringing a blessing to nations which is conspicuously absent in Ezra 9.1–2. The other background which scholars have suggested concerns the purity of animals, foodstuffs and materials such as in Lev. 19.19, 'You shall keep my statutes. You shall not let your animals breed with a different kind; you shall not sow your field with two kinds of seed; nor shall you put on a garment made of two different materials'.

According to the book of Ezra, there was resolve to divorce 'foreign women' according to those 'who tremble at the commandment of our God' and 'done according to the Law' (Ezra 10.2–3). This is most likely an interpretation of the divorce law of Deut. 24.1–4 where a wife may be divorced if the husband finds something 'objectionable', a phrase that was interpreted in many different ways in early Judaism, as we will see in Chapter 4, and interpreted in Ezra to include a reference to divorcing those wives not of the pure seed. This sentiment may also be expressed in the difficult final verse of the book of Ezra (10.44).

Though we are dealing with interpretation and expansion of biblical Law, it is clear that in the book of Ezra these views are deemed authoritative pieces of legal understanding and presumably indistinguishable, as least in terms of authority, from the biblical commandments themselves in the eyes of the author(s). For example, in Ezra 9.14 we read, '. . . shall we break your commandments again and intermarry with the peoples who practise these abominations?' Note Ezra's reaction to the news of the holy seed being mixed in 9.1–2. Ezra tore his garments, pulled out his hair and beard, all a sign of extreme mourning, and sat appalled until the evening sacrifice (Ezra 9.3–4). In Ezra 10.3 Shecaniah believes that sending away Gentile wives and daughters should be 'done according to the law'. In 10.19, those who agreed to dismiss their wives give an offering in the Temple. We might add that the related book of Nehemiah also engages in its own interpretation and expansion of biblical Law (Nehemiah 8, 10). As Nehemiah puts it more generally,

Jeshua, Bani, Sherebiah, Jamin, Akkub, Shabbethai, Hodiah, Maaseiah, Kelita, Azariah, Jozabad, Hanan, Pelaiah, the Levites, helped the people to understand the law, while the people remained in their places. So they read from the book, from the law of God, with interpretation. They gave the sense, so that the people understood the reading. (Neh. 8.7–8)

SECTARIANISM AND LEGAL INTERPRETATION

A crucial period in the development of the interpretation of Jewish Law was ushered in with the Maccabean crisis (c. 167–164 BCE). After interaction with Hellenistic culture in Jerusalem (e.g. building of a gymnasium) and political wrangling with the major international power blocs, the practice of the Law itself was questioned, including Jews apparently prepared to undo the marks of circumcision. In the midst of these controversies, the Seleucid ruler, Antiochus IV, entered Jerusalem and desecrated the Temple. Jewish practices such as circumcision and Sabbath were banned, as were Torah scrolls. This led to the Maccabean revolt, the guerrilla movement headed by Mattathias and his sons, with Mattathias shortly replaced by the famous Judas Maccabeus. The rebels eventually won and rededicated the Temple, the event celebrated at the festival of Hanukkah. This would also lead to the kingdom of ruled the Hasmonean dynasty, a dynasty which would rule independently until the Roman invasion in 63 BCE. The Maccabean crisis and the Hasmonean rule were also controversial in the sense that gave rise to what is usually called 'sectarianism', that is, the rise of groups such as Pharisees, Sadducees and the group at Qumran responsible for the Dead Sea Scrolls perhaps to be identified with the Essenes. The aims of these competing groups were so deeply immersed in both court politics and religious practices that such aims were times indistinguishable.

The stories of martyrdom from the Maccabean crisis can get gruesome and 2 Maccabees, a text recalling the time of the Maccabean crisis and its aftermath, has hints of there being a bodily resurrection for the martyred individual. Most memorably, 2 Maccabees 7 tells the story of a mother and her sons. The sons refuse to eat unclean food and are tortured and killed in a particularly violent fashion. They respond in ways such as the following:

> And when he was at his last breath, he said, 'You accursed wretch, you dismissed us from this present life, but the king of the universe will raise us up to an everlasting renewal of life, because we have died for his laws . . .' 'I got these (hands) from Heaven and because of his laws I disdain them, and from him I hope to get them back again'. (2 Macc. 2.9, 11)

Indeed, it may well be the general context of the Maccabean crisis which explains why a more developed form of life-after-death starts to occur in Jewish literature in its aftermath (e.g. Dan. 12.2–3; 2 Macc. 7; 14.43–46). If the traditional idea of observing the Law was meant to lead to a wealthy and prosperous life, why were people dying for observing the Law? One solution was to extend reward into the afterlife. But one thing is clear after the Maccabean crisis, at least from the perspective of certain Jews: the Law needed to be vigorously defended.

Interpretation of the Law was, unsurprisingly, an issue among the competing groups or 'sects'. The Dead Sea Scrolls provide strong evidence of what was surely the strictest group (the Essenes?) in their attitude towards the Law in early Judaism. Many of the laws may have pre-dated the group, and indeed may not have been initially associated with the group at all, but they were certainly ended up among the Scrolls. The Scrolls expanded and developed the Law to an extent which sometimes made the group very distinct and separate from the rest of Judaism. Some instance of expansion and interpretation of biblical Law should suffice (we will, of course, return to the Scrolls throughout this book):

On 'swarming' or 'creeping' animals, Lev. 11.29–30 says,

These are unclean for you among the creatures that swarm upon the earth: the weasel, the mouse, the great lizard according to its kind, the gecko, the land crocodile, the lizard, the sand lizard, and the chameleon.

In the Damascus Document (CD) these are interpreted to include a variety of small creatures and larvae of bees:

. . . No-one should defile his soul with any living or creeping animal, by eating them, from the larvae of bees to every living being which creeps in water . . . (CD 12.11–13)

On draining blood from animals, Lev. 17.13–14 says,

And anyone of the people of Israel, or of the aliens who reside among them, who hunts down an animal or bird that may be eaten shall pour out its blood and cover it with earth. For the life of every creature – its blood is its life; therefore I have said to the people of Israel: You shall not eat the blood of any creature, for the life of every creature is its blood; whoever eats it shall be cut off.

This is expanded at Qumran to explicitly include fish, perhaps because the writer(s) were confronted with particularly bloody fish (of a larger variety from the Mediterranean?). In other words, fish had to be slaughtered correctly and have the blood drained before they could be eaten. As CD put it,

And fish they should not eat unless they have been opened alive, and their blood poured away. (CD 12.13–14)

The Scrolls expand other laws concerning slaughter of animals. For example, biblical Law prohibits taking the mother creature and her young on the same day:

But you shall not slaughter, from the herd or the flock, an animal with its young on the same day. (Lev. 22.28)

If you come on a bird's nest, in any tree or on the ground, with fledglings or eggs, with the mother sitting on the fledglings or on the eggs, you shall not take the mother with the young. Let the mother go, taking only the young for yourself, in order that it may go well with you and you may live long. (Deut. 22.6–7)

This ruling is expanded and interpreted at Qumran to include, for example, pregnant animals:

. . . And you shall not sacrifice to me a cow, or ewe, or she-goat, which are pregnant, for they are an abomination to me. And you shall not slaughter a cow or a ewe and its young on the same day, and you shall not kill a mother with its young. (11Q19 52.5–7; see also 4Q270 2 ii 15)

In some contexts it is the interpretation of the Law which must override everything. In 4QMMT, a letter outlining that which is deemed correct legal practice, observing their laws appears to be the best approach for the preparation for end times: '. . . we have written to you some works of the Torah which we think are good for you and for your people . . . Reflect on all these matters . . . so that at the end of time, you may rejoice in finding that some of our words are true' (4Q399 14–17 II = 4QMMT C 25–32). So, as with Ezra-Nehemiah, the interpretation of the Law was extremely authoritative. In one document, the Temple Scroll (11QT or 11Q19), we even get God speaking in the first person and thereby giving the re-interpretation of biblical Law as high an authority as can be imagined. For instance, note the way in which the holiness of Temple is extended to Jerusalem: '. . . And a man who lies with his wife and has an ejaculation, for three days shall not enter the whole city of the temple in which I cause my name to dwell. No blind person shall enter it all their days, and they shall not defile the city in whose midst I dwell because I, YHWH, dwell in the midst of the children of Israel for ever and always' (11Q19 45.11–14). Not dissimilarly, in the book of *Jubilees*, a document closely associated with the Dead Sea Scrolls group, has their interpretations of biblical Law linked with Sinai (*Jubilees* 1).

As some of this might imply (notably 4QMMT), by the time of the New Testament the different competing interpretations of biblical Law among various individuals and different groups such as the Pharisees, the Sadducees and the people responsible for the Dead Sea Scrolls, were established. The first century CE Jewish historian, Josephus, describes some legal disagreements between the Pharisees and Sadducees. In one instance, Jonathan the Sadducee had managed to work his ways on John Hyrcanus (134–104 BCE) and so Hyrcanus sided with the Sadducees while deserting the Pharisees by abrogating the regulations which Pharisees had apparently established for the people, and punishing those who observe them (*Ant.* 13.296). According to Josephus, we have another reason for authority of legal understanding – namely, popular support – hence his addition that from this situation grew the hatred of the masses aimed at Hyrcanus and his sons (cf. *Ant.* 13.401–403). Josephus also adds a crucial aside when he explains the differences between the Sadducees and Pharisees:

> . . . the Pharisees have delivered to the people a great many obser-
> vances by succession from their fathers, which are not written in
> the laws of Moses; and for that reason it is that the Sadducees
> reject them, and say that we are to esteem those observances to be
> obligatory which are in the written word, but are not to observe
> what are derived from the tradition of our forefathers. And con-
> cerning these things it is that great disputes and differences have
> arisen among them, while the Sadducees are able to persuade none
> but the rich, and have not the populace favourable to them, but the
> Pharisees have the multitude on their side. (*Ant.* 13.297–298)

Josephus' statement illustrates tendencies and ideas we have seen as early as Ezra-Nehemiah: interpretations and expansions, conflict over interpretation and the importance of popularity.

There are further stories about Pharisees at court and their legal 'traditions', though their influence at court by the time of the New Testament writings seems to have waned, at least according to Josephus (cf. *Ant.* 13.408–409; 14.163–184; 15.1–4, 368–372; 17.41). References to Pharisaic 'tradition' also occur in the New Testament. In Mk 7.1–23, Jesus is portrayed as criticizing the 'tradition of the elders' or 'human tradition' of Pharisees, including examples such as washing hands before meals and immersing various utensils. Notice again the context of conflict and dispute, comparable with the disputes Josephus records between Pharisees and Sadducees. Paul famously claimed to have been, 'as to the Law a Pharisee' (Phil. 3.5) and elsewhere (Gal. 1.13–15) he could also speak of being 'far more zealous for the traditions of my ancestors' while persecuting the church (see also Phil. 3.6), perhaps because of legal issues, though the evidence is far from clear on the nature of the conflict.

After the Jewish revolt against Rome and the fall of the Jerusalem Temple in 70 CE, the rabbinic movement began to emerge in its own right, probably as the successors to the Pharisaic movement, with some emphasis on unity rather than 'sectarianism', though disputes hardly went away. Rabbinic literature is where some of the most famous Jewish expansion and interpretation of the biblical Law takes place, collected in, for instance, the Mishnah, the Tosefta, the Jerusalem/ Palestinian Talmud and the Babylonian Talmud. The Mishnah was compiled around 200 CE and consists of six themed 'orders', each of which contains individual tractates. The themed orders cover a wide range of differing legal opinions on agricultural laws, festival and special days, women, damages, holy things and purity. The Tosefta, similar in thematic structure to the Mishnah – indeed it may have been collected as supplementary material – was edited in the third century CE. The Palestinian Talmud and the Babylonian Talmud were massive expansions of, and commentaries on, much of the material in the Mishnah, with the editing of the Palestinian Talmud dated to the fifth century and the editing of the Babylonian Talmud dating to the sixth century. While much detailed work has been done by scholars such as Jacob Neusner and David Instone-Brewer on establishing pre-70 CE traditions,[2] it is worth re-emphasizing that this material was finally collected much later than the New Testament and must always be used with caution for understanding the Law at the time of the New Testament texts. I remind readers that in this book I will (largely) be using this material in a comparative way as a potential means of understanding New Testament legal texts. Readers can pursue the issue of dating and usefulness themselves should they so wish.

In addition to lengthy individual tractates and passages within the Mishnah, Tosefta, Palestinian Talmud and Babylonian Talmud devoted to issues relevant for present purposes (e.g. Sabbath, purity, tithing), it is notable that the Pharisees turn up in rabbinic literature and are heavily involved in debates about food laws, Sabbath, tithing, purity and so on (e.g. *m. Tohar.* 4.15; *m. Hag.* 2.7; *m. Yad.* 4.6–7; *m. Nid.* 4.2; *m. Parah* 3.7; *t. Shabb.* 1.15; *t. Hag.* 3.35). One of the most famous Pharisees found in rabbinic literature was Hillel (late first century BCE–early first century CE), who is largely portrayed as the effective founder of rabbinic Judaism in rabbinic literature. Hillel and his followers, called the School or House of Hillel, are often contrasted with another Pharisaic faction associated with Shammai and his followers, called the School or House of Shammai. Another notable group which might have been connected with the Pharisaic movement were the 'associates' or *haberim*, although it should be noted that the details of such connections are disputed by some scholars. The *haberim* were particularly associated with observing a particularly strict view of the purity and tithing laws. A key passage concerning the *haberim* is *m. Demai* 2.2–3:

He who undertakes to be trustworthy [one who is assumed to tithe all of his produce] tithes (1) what he eats, and (2) what he sells, and (3) what he purchases, and (4) does not accept the hospitality of a person of the land . . . He who undertakes to be a *haber* (1) does not sell to a person of the land wet or dry [produce, either produce which has been rendered susceptible to impurity or produce which has not been rendered susceptible], and (2) does not purchase from him wet [produce, produce which has been rendered susceptible to impurity . . .

Various Pharisaic and/or rabbinic interpretations are given great authority, with links often given to a great figure from the past, even to the extent, as we saw with the book of *Jubilees*, of attributing their expansions and interpretations to Moses at Sinai:[3]

Said Nahum the Scribe, 'I have received [the following ruling] from R. Miasha, who received [it] from his father, who received [it] from the Pairs, who received [it] from the Prophets, [who received] the law [given] to Moses on Sinai, regarding one who sows his field with two types of wheat . . .' (*m. Peah* 2.6)

Go tell them, 'Do not be anxious about your vote. I have received a tradition from Rabban Yohanan b. Zakkai, who heard it from his teacher, and his teacher from his teacher, a law given to Moses at Sinai, "that Ammon and Moab give poor man's tithe in the Sabbatical year"'. (*m. Yad.* 4.3)

We even get claims such as opposing 'the teachings of the scribes' weighs heavier than opposing 'the teachings of the Torah' (*m. Sanh.* 11.3). In addition to plenty of intra-rabbinic debates over the validity of this or that interpretation (we will return to such issues throughout this book), we also get evidence of different levels of observance of expanded Law, most famously involving the 'people of the land', that is Jews not strictly observant of rabbinic laws (e.g. *m. Dem.*1–2; *m. Aboth* 5.10–19; *m. Sot.* 9.15) or those of the *haberim* (e.g. *m. Dem.* 2–3) or the Pharisaic laws:

The clothing of 'a person of the land' is in the status of midras uncleanness for Pharisees [who eat ordinary food in a state of uncleanness], the clothing of Pharisees is in the status of *midras* uncleanness for those who eat priestly food. The clothing of those who eat heave offering is in the status of *midras* uncleanness for those who eat Holy Things [officiating priests] etc . . . (*m. Hag.* 2.7)

LAW AND IDENTITY

For Jews outside Palestine, the Torah was translated in the Greek (the Septuagint or LXX), a fictional story of which is told in the *Letter of Aristeas*. As happens with translation, interpretative decisions had to be made and even these could reflect legal and cultural decisions. As Sanders points out, food laws were basically the same in the Diaspora but new inclusions were made in the LXX (and Philo) to the list of the ten permitted animals in Deut. 14.4–5, such as the giraffe, while others dropped out from the Hebrew list, such as mountain sheep.

Philo adds more of his own, such as the more localized (in Egypt) cranes and geese (*Spec. Laws* 4.105).[4]

Torah observance, as we will see in Chapter 5, became a flashpoint when Jewish and different Gentile practices came together, particularly in the Jewish Diaspora. The responses to the different cultural contexts in the ancient world varied greatly, from enthusiastic accommodation to hostility.[5] Scholars often talk, sometimes a little too much, about 'boundary markers' associated with the Torah (especially food laws, Sabbath observance and circumcision) which functioned as a means for Jews and outsiders to define who might have been a 'Jew'. The Roman satirist brought some of these 'boundary markers' together with reference to the Law in his not-entirely-kind assessment of Judaism:

> Some who have had a father who reveres the Sabbath, worship nothing but the clouds, and the divinity of the heavens, and see no difference between eating swine's flesh, from which their father abstained, and that of man; and in time they take to circumcision. Having been wont to flout the laws of Rome, they learn and practise and revere the Jewish law, and all that Moses handed down in his secret tome, forbidding to point out the way to any not worshipping the same rites, and conducting none but the circumcised to the desired fountain. For all which the father was to blame, who gave up every seventh day to idleness, keeping it apart from all the concerns of life. (Juvenal, *Satires* 14.96–106)

Philo, the first century Jewish philosopher based in Alexandria, wrote extensively on the significance of the Law, partly in response to criticism of those practices deemed Jewish. In contrast to Juvenal, Philo can only gasp in awe at the wonders of the Law and its pervasive influence in a slightly optimistic assessment:

> But this is not so entirely wonderful, although it may fairly by itself be considered a thing of great intrinsic importance, that his

laws were kept securely and immutably from all time; but this is more wonderful by far, as it seems, that not only the Jews, but that also almost every other nation, and especially those who make the greatest account of virtue, have dedicated themselves to embrace and honour them, for they have received this especial honour above all other codes of laws, which is not given to any other code . . . our laws which Moses has given to us . . . influence all nations, barbarians and Greeks, the inhabitants of continents and islands, the eastern nations and the western, Europe and Asia; in short, the whole habitable world from one extremity to the other. (*Mos.* 2.17, 20)

Philo was extremely comfortable with Hellenistic philosophy which was able to underpin such grandiose assessments of Jewish Law and in a related way meant that Jewish laws could be allegorized to reflect certain virtues and principles. However, Philo makes a significant qualification in terms of his construction of Jewish identity because, unlike some, he famously would *not* take the allegorical meaning to one logical conclusion and remove the physical implications of the commandments:

For there are some men, who, looking upon written laws as symbols of things appreciable by the intellect . . . But now men living solitarily by themselves as if they were in a desert, or else as if they were mere souls unconnected with the body . . . overlook what appears to the many to be true, and seek for plain naked truth by itself . . . For although the seventh day is a lesson to teach us the power which exists in the uncreated God, and also that the creature is entitled to rest from his labours, it does not follow that on that account we may abrogate the laws which are established respecting it, so as to light a fire, or till land, or carry burdens, or bring accusations, or conduct suits at law, or demand a restoration of a deposit, or exact the repayment of a debt, or do any other of the things which are usually permitted at times which are not days of festival . . . nor because the rite of circumcision is an emblem of the excision of pleasures and of all the passions, and of the destruction of that impious opinion, according to which the mind has imagined itself to be by itself competent to produce offspring, does it follow that we are to annul the law which has been enacted about circumcision . . . But it is right to think that this class of things resembles the body, and the other class the soul; therefore, just as we take care of the body because it is the abode of the soul, so also must we take care of the laws that are enacted in plain terms: for while they are regarded, those other things also will be more clearly understood, of which these laws are the symbols . . . (*Migr.* 89–93)

Of course, identity is a matter of perspective and no doubt those adhering to allegorizing alone saw themselves as Jewish but, from Philo's perspective, it was also the physical performance of the commandments (e.g. Sabbath observance) that remained crucial. Otherwise, from this perspective, how can a Jew be a Jew if shut off from the outward manifestations of Jewish identity performed by the community?

Using the Torah to emphasize Jewish identity could be done in different ways, some more confrontational than others. We have already seen such issues arising in the context of the Maccabean crisis where Jews were remembered as dying heroically for the Law. It is probably significant that Josephus claims that the Pharisees were 'influential among townsfolk' and that their sacred rites were followed by the inhabitants of the cities (*Ant.* 18.15). By the first century we know that several towns in and around Palestine were influenced by Hellenistic culture such as the building of theatres and Herod's introduction of four-yearly games in honour of Caesar (*Ant.* 15.268). Yet, from one Jewish perspective, this might lead to another Maccabean crisis which gives reasons to uphold Jewish identity focused on Torah observance over against the perceived lawlessness of Gentile culture. In this context, it may well have been that the Pharisees would have been visible adherents of Jewish traditions in the face of the perceived threat of Gentile culture.[6]

Josephus gives us several first century Palestinian examples of the combustible elements involved with the Torah under imperialism. One example might be when Caesar's slave Stephen was robbed by Jewish bandits. Troops attempted to find the culprits in the villages en route to Beth Horon and one soldier committed the provocative act of burning a copy of the Torah. The resulting uproar led to the procurator pacifying the outraged by ordering the execution of the soldier (*War* 2.231; cf. *Ant.* 20.113–115). Arguably the most prominent pre-Jewish war example is the Emperor Gaius Caligula's attempt to place a statute of himself in the Temple. According to Josephus, some Jews promised a harvest of banditry if the threat was carried out (*Ant.* 18.269–275) and brings up the issue of Torah observances: 'the Jews appealed to their law and the custom of their ancestors, and pleaded that they were forbidden to place an image of God, much more of a man, not only in the sanctuary but even in any unconsecrated spot throughout the country' (*War* 2.195). The context of the Jewish revolt against Rome in 66–70 CE provides an obvious broader context for particularly confrontational uses. One revolutionary figure called Jesus was furious when he believed that Josephus (the historian himself) was going to side with Rome. According to Josephus, Jesus' speech was popular and it would seem that the role of the Torah played a significant part in Jesus' rhetorical posturing:

> With a copy of the laws of Moses in his hands, he now stepped forward and said: 'If you cannot, for your own sakes, citizens, detest Josephus, fix your eyes on your country's laws, which your commander-in-chief intended to betray, and for their sakes hate the crime and punish the audacious criminal'. (*Life* 134–35; cf. *Life* 66)

In a not dissimilar way, some Jewish writers could tie in a message of social justice (of course part of the Law too) with their reading of the Law. Indeed, one notable theme which emerges in early Jewish texts is that oppression is carried out by those who do not observe the Law as they ought to (from the perspective of a given writer) or by Gentiles, deemed beyond the Law by default. The Dead Sea Scrolls give some particularly ferocious examples. CD, for instance, is immersed in language about the Law (including the classic idea of Law and 'walking' on the correct path):

> The princes of Judah are those upon whom the rage will be vented, for they hope to be healed but the defects stick (to them); all are rebels because they have not left the path of traitors and have defiled themselves in paths of licentiousness, and with wicked wealth, avenging themselves, and each one bearing resentment against his brother, and each one hating his fellow. Each one became obscured by blood relatives, and approached for debauchery and bragged about wealth and gain. Each one did what was right in his eyes and each one has chosen the stubbornness of his heart. They did not keep apart from the people and have rebelled with insolence, walking on the path of the wicked ones, about whom God says: 'Their wine is serpents' venom and cruel poisons of asps'. (CD 8.3–10)

From such perspectives, then, avoidance of social injustice can be done by what is perceived correct interpretation of the Law. From a different context, the following may well reflect this kind of thinking in early Judaism:

> And there will be no spirit of error of Beliar any more, for he will be thrown into fire for ever . . . And those that are in penury for the Lord's sake will be made rich and those who are in want will eat their fill and those who are weak will be made strong . . . And so, my children, observe the whole of the law of the Lord, for there is hope for all who make straight their way. (*T. Jud.* 25.3–26.1)

The idea of wealth leading to sin is found in early Judaism and is tied in closely with Law observance as the way to avoid such sin (e.g. 4Q171 2.9–16; *T. Jud.* 25.3–26.1). This line of thought is also found in the Gospels. Mark 10.17–31 is the story of a rich man who has observed a list of commandments but needs to supplement this by selling his properties and giving the proceeds to the poor.[7] The commandments listed in the passage include the Markan Jesus' own expansion of the Law by adding a prohibition of defrauding (Mk 10.19) to the Ten Commandments (cf. Exod. 20.17/Deut. 5.21) and when this sort of language is used elsewhere it has strong implications of not withholding workers' wages and avoidance of exploitation (see e.g. Deut. 24.14–15; Mal. 3.5; Sir. 4.1; 1QapGen 20.11; *Tg. Onq.* Lev. 5.21; *Tg. Ps.–J.* Lev. 5.23; *Tg. Neof.* and *Ps–J.* Deut. 24.14; *Tg.* Mal. 3.5; *Lev. R.* 12.1). Presumably a key reason for this addition was that Jesus was in dialogue with a rich man, precisely the kind of person who could defraud.

Despite the rich man claiming to have observed the commandments, including the new one not to defraud, Jesus still severely downplays the rich man's chances of entering the kingdom of God with the famous saying, 'It is easier for a camel to go through the eye of a needle than for someone who is rich to enter the kingdom of God' (Mk 10.25). What this passage seems to be doing is following a Jewish tradition which rejects the interpretation that wealth and prosperity in the here and now as a result of observing the commandments (cf. Deut. 28.1–14; Job 1.10; 42.10; Isa. 3.10; Prov. 10.22; Tob. 12.9; Sir. 3.1, 6; 25.7–11; 35.13; 44.10–15; 51.27–30; Bar. 4.1) and places reward in the life to come (cf. Mk 10.29–31; Dan. 12; 2 Macc. 7; *1 En.* 92–105). Another Jewish text knows that the view of riches as a reward in the here and now is a problem so it attacks such a view vigorously:

Woe to you, you sinners! For your money makes you appear like the righteous, but your hearts do reprimand you like real sinners, this very matter shall be a witness against you, as a record of your evil . . . When you are dead in the wealth of your sins. Those who are like you will say of you, 'Happy are you sinners! (The sinners) have seen all their days. They have died now in prosperity and wealth. They have not experienced struggle and battle in their lifetime. You yourselves know that they will bring your souls down to Sheol; and they shall experience evil and great tribulation – in darkness, nets, and burning flame . . .' (*1 En.* 96.4; 103.5–8)

The Markan Jesus also fits into that view whereby wealth gets equated with wickedness (see e.g. CD 4.15–19; 1QS 11.1–2; *Ps. Sol.* 5.16) and where you cannot serve God and Mammon (Lk. 16.13/Mt. 6.24). As an earlier Jewish text put it, 'if one is excessively rich, he sins' (*Ps. Sol.* 5.16).

The interpretation of the Torah against those deemed rich is found elsewhere in the Gospels, most starkly in the parable of the Rich Man and Lazarus. Here the destitute Lazarus and the opulence of the rich man are obvious polar opposites. In the afterlife, however, their positions were reversed: the poor Lazarus gets to be with Abraham while the rich man suffers fiery torments. There is only one reason given for this utter reversal of fortunes and that is found in Lk. 16.25: 'Child, remember that during your lifetime you received your good things, and Lazarus in like manner evil things; but now he is comforted here, and you are in agony'. When the rich man wants to warn his brothers they should not need any warning because it is all there in scripture. The parable concludes,

He said, 'Then, father, I beg you to send him to my father's house – for I have five brothers – that he may warn them, so that they will not also come into this place of torment'. Abraham replied, 'They have Moses and the prophets; they should listen to them'. He [the rich man] said, 'No, father Abraham; but if someone goes to them from the dead, they will repent'. He said to him, 'If they do not listen to Moses and the prophets, neither will they be convinced even if someone rises from the dead'. (Lk. 16.27–31)

This should not be understood as a reference to the resurrection for the simple reason that Lazarus and not Jesus is the one to be sent back in the way that other figures could be sent back from the dead to warn the living (cf. 1 Sam. 28.7–20; *Eccl. Rab.* 9.10.1–2).[8] Here, again, we have the Torah understood to be interpreted from the perspective of the destitute and those deemed poor and against those deemed wealthy.

SUMMARY

There is far, far more that could be said about the details and the trends in early Jewish legal interpretation. To re-emphasize: this chapter is only a brief overview of some of the issues pertinent for the study of the New Testament. In addition to the importance some Jews and some non-Jews attached to the Torah as a crucial part of Jewish identity, we have seen that by the time of the New Testament, development and expansion of the biblical commandments was in full swing. As early as Ezra and Nehemiah we can see application and creative interpretation to fit new historical and social circumstances, most notoriously with the issue of mixed marriages and the pure ethnic seed. With the Maccabean crisis came the emergence of various groups at least partly dedicated to the understanding, expansion and development of the Law in different social and historical circumstances. It seems clear that such groups were liable to fall out and engage in some heated debate, perhaps even violent debate, over the nature of legal interpretation. One of these groups, the Pharisees, appear to have been some kind of descendants of those responsible for the emerging rabbinic movement which has left us with masses of legal material, much of which is of at least thematic relevance for comparison with the New Testament. With these general ideas in mind, we can now turn to more precise legal topics.

CHAPTER 2

SABBATH

He [Jesus] respects the Sabbath not because it means going to church but because it represents a temporary escape from the burden of labor. The Sabbath is about resting not religion. One of the best reasons for being a Christian, as for being a socialist, is that you don't like having to work, and reject the fearful idolatry of it so rife in countries like the United States. Truly civilized societies do not hold predawn power breakfasts.

Terry Eagleton[1]

We could, of course, add 'Jew' to 'Christian' and 'socialist' in the quotation from Eagleton because Sabbath is a well known day of rest for Jews, as Eagleton implies when speaking of Jesus. In basic terms the Jewish day of rest from work is, roughly speaking, Saturday. More precisely, the day of rest extends from 'from [Friday] evening to [Saturday] evening' (Lev. 23.32; cf. Neh. 13.19). The observance within this time frame appears to be assumed in Mk 1.32: 'That evening, at sundown, they brought to him all who were sick or possessed with demons'. In other words the people waiting until the Sabbath was finished before they carried burdens (see below). The Dead Sea Scrolls retain an extremely precise definition of timing: 'No-one should do work on the sixth day, from the moment when the sun's disc is at a distance of its diameter from the gate, for this is what he said: "Observe the Sabbath day to keep it holy" (Deut. 5.12)' (CD 10.14–17).

THE DAY OF REST FROM 'WORK'

The key foundational texts for Sabbath observance are Exod. 20.8–11 and Deut. 5.12–15, both in versions of the Ten Commandments. There is a subtle difference between the two. In Exod. 20.8–11, the Sabbath is grounded in God's activity in Creation: 'For in six days the Lord made heaven and earth, the sea and all that is in them, but rested the seventh day; therefore the Lord blessed the Sabbath day and consecrated it' (20.11). In others words, Jews are to rest just like God did when he created the world. Similar sentiment is emphasized in Exod. 31.12–17 where the Sabbath commandment is also, like circumcision, a sign of the covenant; it is an indication of the relationship between God and Israel. In Deut. 5.12–15, the Sabbath is grounded in God's action in the Exodus: 'Remember that you were a slave in the land of Egypt, and the Lord your God brought you out from there with a mighty hand and an outstretched arm; therefore the Lord your God commanded you to keep the Sabbath day' (5.15). Notice also that in the Ten Commandments the Sabbath is a day of rest for the whole of society, the slave, the animal, the child and the resident alien. Everyone in such contexts has the right to the day off work. The first century CE Jewish philosopher, Philo, extends this broad view of society to include nature itself and grounded in a seemingly unusual principle 'no one shall touch':

> For the rest extends also to every herd and to whatever was made for the service of man, like slaves serving him who is by nature their master. It extends also to every kind of tree and plant, for it does not allow us to cut a shoot, branch or even a leaf, or to pluck any fruit whatsoever. They are all released and as it were have freedom on that day, under the general proclamation that no one shall touch. (*Life of Moses* 2.22)

But the broad view of society needs qualification. The Sabbath commandment was, of course, given to the Israelites at Sinai/Horeb. However, there are different emphases when it comes to Gentiles observing the Sabbath. In the foundational commandment the issue appears only to a small extent: the resident alien is permitted to observe the commandment, though so are animals. Isaiah has some very positive things to say about Gentiles, including comments, for example, in the context of Sabbath observance: 'And the foreigners who join themselves to the Lord, to minister to him, to love the name of the Lord, and to be his servants, all who keep the Sabbath, and do not profane, and hold fast my covenant – these I will bring to my holy mountain, and make them joyful in my house of prayer . . .' (Isa. 56.6–7). In the eschatological future, 'From new moon to new moon, and from Sabbath to Sabbath, all flesh shall come to worship before me, says the Lord' (Isa. 66.23). Around the time of the New Testament texts, it appears as if there were Gentiles who were attracted to the idea of a day of rest. As Josephus puts it, though not a little over-optimistically, humanity

> . . . had a great inclination of a long time to follow our religious observances; for there is not any city of the Greeks, nor any of the barbarians, nor any nation whatever, where our custom of resting on the seventh day has not come, and by which our fasts and light-ing lamps, and many of our prohibitions as to our food, are not observed. (*Apion* 2.282)

The Roman satirist Juvenal, in a famous text we saw in the previous chapter, also suggests certain Gentiles were attracted to the Sabbath rest but he is not so happy about this: 'Some who have had a father who reveres the Sabbath . . . Having been wont to flout the laws of Rome, they learn and practise and revere the Jewish law . . . For all which the father was to blame, who gave up every seventh day to idleness, keeping it apart from all the concerns of life' (Juvenal, *Satires* 14.96–106). On the other hand, there were Jews who thought Gentiles should not observe the Sabbath. According to *Jubilees*, a text dating back to the second century BCE: ' . . . the creator of all things blessed it, but he did not hallow all peoples and nations to keep Sabbath on it, but Israel only: them alone on earth did he allow to eat

and drink and keep Sabbath on it' (*Jub*. 2.31). This Jewish only ordi-
nance is also found in rabbinic literature, as in the following example
which deals with the problem of the banned act of carrying a burden
on the Sabbath (see further below):

If a Jew is journeying on the eve of the Sabbath and is overtaken
by nightfall and he has in his hand money or any other object, how
shall he act? The Rabbis have learnt as follows: If nightfall over-
takes a man on the road [on Friday] he hands over his purse to
a non-Jew. And why is it permissible to hand over one's purse to a
non-Jew? Levi said: When the children of Noah were charged
[to observe certain laws], they were given seven Laws only, the
observance of Sabbath not being one of them; therefore have the
Rabbis permitted a Jew to hand over objects to a non-Jew. R. Jose
b. Hanina said: a non-Jew who observes the Sabbath whilst he
is uncircumcised incurs liability for the punishment of death.
Why? Because [non-Jews] were not commanded concerning it . . .
R. Hiyya b. Abba said in the name of R. Johanan . . . the Sabbath
is a [reunion] between Israel and God, as it is said, *It is a sign
between Me and the children of Israel* (Exod. 31.17); therefore any
non-Jew who, being uncircumcised, thrusts himself between them
incurs the penalty of death . . . (*Deut. R.* 1.21)

According to biblical Law, the Sabbath could be described as God's
gift to his people: 'See! The Lord has given you the Sabbath' (Exod.
16.29). There is a similar rabbinic saying attributed to R. Simeon ben
Menasya and presented in the context of the general idea that saving
life overrides the Sabbath (see below), 'The Sabbath is delivered to
you and you are not delivered to the Sabbath' (*Mek. Exod.* 31.12–17;
cf. *b. Yoma* 85b). This sentiment is also found prior to the New Testament in *Jub*. 2.17: 'he gave us a great sign, the Sabbath day, so that
we might work six days and observe a Sabbath from all work on the
seventh day'. We clearly have a similar sentiment attributed to Jesus
in Mk 2.27–28: Then he said to them, 'The Sabbath was made for
humankind and not humankind for the Sabbath; so the Son of Man is

lord even of the Sabbath'. It is worth pointing out that this might be a literal translation of the Aramaic idiom 'son of man' which can refer both to speaker and a broader group of people. If so, Mk 2.27–28 would be a piece of classic parallelism whereby the general sentiment of the Sabbath as a gift to humanity is repeated in 2.28 but also with reference to Jesus defending the actions of his disciples plucking grain on the Sabbath (Mk 2.23–26) as part of that gift. In the parallel versions in Lk. 6.1–6 and Mt. 12.1–8, Mark's generalizing 'The Sabbath was made for humankind, and not humankind for the Sabbath' is dropped, presumably designed to make Jesus the supreme legal interpreter and remove the generalizing reading of 'son of man' by making the phrase a title for Jesus alone.

As this might already imply, it is one thing to say avoid work on the Sabbath but another to precisely define what 'work' actually is. In biblical Law work includes 'ploughing time and harvest time' (Exod. 34.21) and Israelites must not kindle a fire in any dwelling (Exod. 35.2). Outside the Pentateuch, Amos 8.5 mentions merchants avoiding the selling of grain and wheat on the Sabbath even if, according to Amos, they cannot wait for the Sabbath to be finished in order to make a profit and exploit the poor. Jeremiah 17.19–27 opposes commercial activity on the Sabbath with the famous prohibition, 'Thus says the Lord: For the sake of your lives, take care that you do not bear a burden on the Sabbath day or bring it in by the gates of Jerusalem. And do not carry a burden out of your houses on the Sabbath or do any work . . .' (Jer. 17.21–22).

According to Nehemiah 13, it appears that people were acting in direct contradiction to the commandment not to work and in direct contradiction to Jeremiah's prohibition of carrying burdens on the Sabbath. People were 'treading wine presses on the Sabbath, and bringing in heaps of grain and loading them on donkeys; and also wine, grapes, figs and all kinds of burdens, which they brought into Jerusalem on the Sabbath day; and I warned them at that time against selling food. Tyrians also, who lived in the city, brought in fish and all kinds of merchandise and sold them on the Sabbath to the people of Judah, and in Jerusalem' (Neh. 13.15). Nehemiah was not pleased so he rebuked the nobles of Judah: 'What is this evil thing that you are doing, profaning the Sabbath day?' (Neh. 13.17) So it is clear that all these activities ought to be banned on the Sabbath for Nehemiah and Nehemiah does just that. Just before the Sabbath the gates of Jerusalem were to be shut and reopened when the Sabbath was over. Guards were put in place to prevent any burdens from being brought in on the Sabbath and merchants were intimidated.

This background may shed light on one of the references to the Sabbath in the fifth century BCE Aramaic documents from Elephantine in Egypt. It *may* be the case that this unorthodox Jewish military community observed the restriction of commercial activity and *possibly* even the prohibition of carrying of a burden. Someone called Uriah mentions a shipment that needs to arrive before the Sabbath.[2]

In the healing story of Jn 5.1–18 it looks as if there is a dispute, among other things, over carrying a burden in general rather than simply the more specific reasons given in Jeremiah, Nehemiah and Elephantine. Jesus says to the would-be healed man, 'Stand up, take your mat and walk'. And then healed man took up his mat and walked. John then gives the crucial information to contextualize the response of 'the Jews': 'Now that day was a Sabbath. So the Jews said to the man who had been cured, "It is the Sabbath; it is not lawful for you to carry your mat"' (Jn 5.8–10). A similar generalizing frame of reference for carrying a burden, rather than simply an economic frame of reference, is reflected in Mk 1.32 where the people reflect the view of 'the Jews' of John's Gospel in that there is waiting for sundown and the end of the Sabbath before carrying the sick. In other words, there is the assumption that carrying sick people not acceptable on the Sabbath.

In early Judaism, the avoidance of carrying a burden out of a house appears to have been followed, at least in major texts, and in some very creative ways. *Jubilees* simply reiterates: 'And they shall not bring in or take out anything from one house to another on that day [the Sabbath] . . . ' (*Jub*. 2.30). Perhaps most famously, the issue of carrying a burden out of a house was an issue of some controversy between Pharisees and Sadducees. As ever, we might want to think of the discussion in terms of a question arising out of a new situation: what if you want to eat with friends nearby? One ingenious solution was to think of ways in which it was understood that one courtyard could be interwoven with another courtyard so that the two court-yards become one (generally called an *'erub*) and so any problems of carrying food from one household to another household were effectively overcome. There is a rabbinic tractate called *'Erubin* dedi-cated to such issues and it thereby allowed different households to celebrate the Sabbath together. It also seems as if the Sadducees were associated with a position that did not accept such a concept, at least it appears to be assumed in the following passage: 'Said Rabban Gamaliel, "A Sadducean lived with us in the same alleyway in Jerusalem. And father said to us, 'Make haste and bring all sorts of utensils into the alleyway before he brings out his and prohibits you [from carrying about in it]'"' (*m. 'Erub.* 6.2).

PRECISELY WHAT IS 'WORK'?

In terms of precise definitions of what constituted 'work' in early Judaism, we find a range of suggestions. One of the most famous definitions of work from early Judaism is the rabbinic 39 prohibitions (*m. Shab.* 7.2) which include, grinding, shearing wool, weaving, tying and untying, hunting and preparing a deer, building, hitting with a hammer and so on. The Damascus Document (CD), found among the Dead Sea Scrolls, lays out a range of practices which constitute 'work'. In CD 10–12 we have prohibitions of, for instance, saying a useless or stupid word, lending, speaking about the next day's work, sending a foreigner to do work in place, open a sealed vessel, helping an animal give birth, using a rope or utensil to help someone who has fallen into a place of water and so on. Whereas the Mishnah rulings may look to many of us like fairly obvious expansions to include different types of work, the CD rulings are more precise still in ways that do not always seem like obvious cases of work and contain cases of future work even if no present work is actually being carried out.

On the subject of animals, there were some fairly strict rulings, such as CD 11.12–13: 'No-one should help an animal give birth on the Sabbath. And if (it falls) into a well or a pit, he should not take it out on the Sabbath'. This appears to have been a radical view. Mt. 12.11–12 argues that animals may be assisted on the Sabbath and assumes a position with which the opponents of Jesus would agree: 'Suppose one of you has only one sheep and it falls into a pit on the Sabbath; will you not lay hold of it and lift it out? How much more valuable is a human being than a sheep! So it is lawful to do good on the Sabbath'. At the very least we have echoes of a similar position from later rabbinic literature: 'They do not deliver the young of cattle on the festival, but they help out' (*m. Shabb.* 18.3). Clearly, then, Jesus (or the Lukan Jesus), Pharisees and later rabbinic literature can make assumptions that animals can be helped on the Sabbath, a view unsurprisingly practical in a largely agrarian world. To highlight the radical nature of CD, animals were not the only ones who could suffer if they fell into dangerous places; humans too. So CD 11.16, 'And any living man who falls into a place of water or into a <reservoir>, no-one should take him out with a ladder or rope or a utensil'. That this was also an extreme view is shown by the common view that any doubt about saving life, which, as we will see, includes related contexts much less dangerous than those proposed by CD, always overrules the Sabbath.

We might also note that Josephus refers to the Sabbath practices of the Essenes which have close similarities with CD, perhaps no surprise if the Essenes were behind a text such as CD: 'they are stricter than any other of the Jews in resting from their labours on the seventh day; for they not only get their food ready the day before, that they may not be obliged to kindle a fire on that day, but they will not move any vessel out of its place, nor go to stool thereon' (*War* 2.147). *Jubilees* is likewise similar to CD in many ways. A notable parallel is that both CD and *Jubilees* (50.8) do not allow speaking about matters of work or of the task to be carried out on the following day. *Jubilees* provides numerous Sabbath prohibitions (*Jub.* 2.17–33; 50.6–13). In addition to those just noted and those in Scripture, these prohibitions include: avoiding sex on the Sabbath (because this is work!), tilling the field, loading an animal, travelling by ship, hunting and slaughtering an animal, war and so on. Notice, as ever, that this is believed to be a view which is as authoritative as possible: '. . . the man who does any of these things on the Sabbath shall die, so that the sons of Israel may observe the Sabbaths in accordance with the commandments concerning the Sabbath of the land, as it is written on the tablets which he gave into my hands to write out for you the laws of the seasons . . .' (50.13).

Of particular relevance to Mk 2.23–28 and parallels – the dispute over Jesus' disciples plucking grain on the Sabbath – is the following prohibition from the Damascus Document: 'No-one is to eat on the Sabbath day except what has been prepared; and from what is lost in the field he should not eat, nor should he drink except of what there is in the camp' (CD 10.22–23). It seems as if only food prepared before the Sabbath can be eaten and this includes a prohibition of anything edible which has dropped to the floor in a field. There are similar lines of thinking elsewhere in early Judaism. From the book of *Jubilees*, which has some close connections with the people responsible for the Dead Sea Scrolls, we read: '. . . they [the sons of Israel] should not prepare on it [the Sabbath] anything to eat or drink that they have not prepared for themselves already in their homes on the sixth day' (*Jub.* 2.29). In the above cited passage from Philo, recall that plucking fruit was not permitted on the otherwise unknown principle that 'no one should touch'. Presumably someone like Philo would have sided with the scribes and Pharisees against Jesus and his disciples in the debate over plucking grain recorded in Mk 2.23–28. From later rabbinic literature we have a passage which potentially illuminates the dispute in Mk 2.23–28 and parallels: 'Six rules did the men of Jericho make . . . For three the Sages criticized them . . . [2] they eat on the Sabbath fruit which had fallen under a tree . . .'

(m. *Pesahim* 4.8). If there is a connection between the Pharisees and the early rabbis then this passage further explains why (the Markan) Jesus was questioned about the behaviour of his disciples. From the perspective of Jesus' opponents, plucking grain was something close to 'work', even though 'plucking' is not more precisely recorded as being an issue until the time of the Tosefta (*t. Shab.* 9.17; cf. *y. Shab.* 7.2), though even here it is not technically plucking grain.

However, notice that *m. Pesahim* 4.8 implies that there are two sides to the story. Clearly the 'men of Jericho' thought it acceptable on the Sabbath to eat fruit which had fallen under a tree. Here we are in the territory of disputes over *interpretation* or *expansion* of biblical Law because we should not forget that there is no biblical prohibition of picking up fruit, or indeed plucking grain, on the Sabbath. In fact early rabbinic literature shows that debates over what constituted 'work' were still recorded despite the 39 prohibitions. The first century House of Shammai, for example, was recorded as not permitting nets spread to catch animals, birds, or fish unless there was time for them to be caught *before* the Sabbath, whereas the House of Hillel permitted it (*m. Shab.* 1.6). A certain Rabbi Eleazar was involved in disputes over details of Sabbath observance, as indeed he was over various interpretations of the Law. According to another passage from the tractate *Shabbat*, 'Honeycombs which one broke on the eve of the Sabbath and [the honey] came out on its own – they are prohibited. R. Eleazar permits [the use of honey on the Sabbath]' (*m. Shab.* 22.1) Similarly, one Eliezer is reported to have said that if someone scraped honey from a beehive on the Sabbath he is culpable whereas the Sages disagreed (*m. Sheb.* 10.7/*m. 'Uq.* 3.10).

It is worth noting that Christianity would eventually not become associated with Sabbath observance and shift the idea of the 'Lord's Day' to Sunday. Such issues were certainly present in the first century and no doubt were a significant contribution to Christians identifying themselves over against Judaism and non-Christians identifying Christianity as something distinctive from Judaism. Most notably, in Romans it seems that Paul tries to bring together those still observing the Sabbath and those no longer observing the Sabbath: 'Some judge one day to be better than another, while others judge all days to be alike. Let all be fully convinced in their own minds. Those who observe the day, observe it in honour of the Lord' (Rom. 14.5–6). In more polemical contexts, Paul seems to be alluding to Sabbath observance and does not appear to be in favour of it if it means placing too much emphasis on it in terms of salvation and identity: 'Now, however, that you have come to know God, or rather to be known by God, how can you turn back again to the weak and beggarly elemental spirits? How can you want to be enslaved to them again? You are observing special days, and months, and seasons, and years. I am afraid that my work for you may have been wasted' (Gal. 4.9–11). This may not be too far removed from the sentiments in Romans when Paul says that if it is to be observed in a Christian context it is done in honour of the Lord. But from this perspective, the importance of dedication to Sabbath observance has effectively been undermined as it is still no longer *required*. Whether written by Paul or not, this is effectively confirmed in Colossians: 'Therefore do not let anyone condemn you in matters of food and drink or of observing festivals, new moons, or Sabbaths. Which are a shadow of things to come; but the body is of Christ . . .' (Col. 2.16–17).

EXEMPTIONS

Although there were disputed details, there were also widely held exemptions from the prohibition of 'work'. Priests, for instance, had to work on the Sabbath and this is rooted in biblical Law. Numbers 28.9–10 commands the following: 'On the Sabbath day: two male lambs a year old without blemish, and two tenths of an ephah of choice flour for a grain offering, mixed with oil, and its drink offering – this is the burnt offering for every Sabbath, in addition to the regular burnt offering and its drink offering'. Surely this was work, and surely the priests deserve stoning to death by the logic of biblical Sabbath Law (Num. 15.32–36)! Emphatically not, say early Jewish sources. Yes, priestly activity on the Sabbath was technically 'work' but it was an acceptable exception. In *Jubilees* we get a strong defence of the priestly activity:

> . . . rest on it from all the work men have to do, except burn frank-incense and present offerings and sacrifices in the Lord's presence every day and every Sabbath. This work alone shall be done on the Sabbath days in the sanctuary of the Lord your God. (*Jub.* 50.10–11)

Similarly in the Damascus Document we get the following: 'No-one should offer anything upon the altar on the Sabbath, except the sacrifice of the Sabbath, for it is thus written, "except your offerings of the Sabbath" [Lev. 23.38]' (CD 11.17–18). In Matthew's version of the dispute over plucking grain on the Sabbath we find an additional argument used to defend the disciples' actions which assume the validity of priestly work: '. . . have you not read in the law that on the Sabbath the priests in the Temple break the Sabbath and yet are guiltless?' (Mt. 12.5).

In the dispute over plucking of grain, Mark (followed by Matthew and Luke) also mentions the actions of a hungry David and his companions (1 Sam. 21) in relation to priestly activity: 'He [David] entered the house of God, when Abiathar was high priest, and ate the bread of the Presence, which it is not lawful for any but the priests to eat, and he gave some to his companions' (Mk 2.26). While not mentioned explicitly by Mark, and no doubt assumed, this refers to some of the priestly activities on the Sabbath. The 'bread of the presence', or 'shewbread', is changed on the Sabbath and eaten by priests. As Leviticus puts it, 'Every Sabbath day he will arrange it before the Lord continually on behalf of the children of Israel as an eternal covenant. And it will be for Aaron and for his sons and they will eat it in a holy place' (Lev. 24.8–9). Josephus gives us further detail of this priestly Sabbath practice where the bread of the Presence is changed every Sabbath:

> . . . they were baked the day before the Sabbath, but were brought into the holy place on the morning of the Sabbath, and set upon the

holy table, six on a heap, one loaf still standing opposite one another; where two golden cups full of frankincense were also set upon them, and there they remained till another Sabbath, and then other loaves were brought in their stead, while the loaves were given to the priests for their food, and the frankincense was burnt in that sacred fire wherein all their offerings were burnt also; and so other frankincense was set upon the loaves instead of what was there before. (*Ant.* 3.255–256; cf. 1 Chron. 9.32; *m. Sukk.* 5.7–8; *m. Menah.* 11.7; *b. Pesah.* 47a)

A prominent exception to working on the Sabbath was made in the case of danger to life. According to *m. Yoma* 8.6, 'Further did R. Mattiah b. Harash say, "He who has a pain in his throat – they drop medicine into his mouth on the Sabbath, because it is a matter of doubt as to danger to life. And any matter of doubt as to a danger to life overrides the prohibitions of the Sabbath"'. This principle of saving life – or even any doubts concerning danger to life – was known long before the Mishnah. It appears that Mk 3.4 shows awareness of the principle of saving life in the context of Jesus' healings: 'Is it lawful to do good or to do harm on the Sabbath, to save life or to kill?' This principle seems to have been developed even earlier, around the time of the Maccabean crisis. Antiochus' commander, Apollonius, went to Jerusalem and pretended that he had peaceful intentions. He simply waited until the Sabbath before massacring large amounts of people. Judas Maccabeus and his gang escaped and lived in the wild (2 Macc. 5.24–27). According to the story, Mattathias, Judas Maccabeus' father, realized that some alternative decision had to be taken otherwise the situation was going to get desperate:

If we do as our kindred have done and refuse to fight with the gentiles for our lives and for our ordinances, they will quickly destroy us from the earth. (1 Macc. 2.40)

This is the decision they made: 'Let us fight against anyone who comes to attack us on the Sabbath day; let us not die as our kindred died in their hiding places' (1 Macc. 2.41). However, not everybody necessarily accepted this logic. We might recall *Jub.* 50.12–13: '. . . any man who does work on it . . . who fasts or makes war on the day of the Sabbath, let the man who does any of these on the day of the Sabbath die'. However, fighting if attacked does appear to have been a widespread view in early Judaism. When the Romans under Pompey attacked Jerusalem in 63 BCE they did not attack on the Sabbath because, as Josephus comments, 'the Jews only acted defensively on Sabbath days'. Instead, in a smart move, the Romans set up their military machinery which they otherwise would not have been able to do on any other day without the obligatory retaliation (*War* 1.145–147).

If 'work' has to be defined then perhaps it is no surprise that danger to life was interpreted in different ways. Moreover, rabbinic literature even allows ways of healing by default if certain healing methods are not permitted on the Sabbath. In the following passage, direct application of the medicinal is not allowed but if it just so happened that the medicinal were included in a more mundane practice . . .

He who is concerned about his teeth may not suck vinegar through them. But he dunks [his bread] in the normal way, and if he is healed, he is healed. He who is concerned about his loins [which give him pain], he may not anoint them with wine or vinegar. But he anoints with oil – not with rose oil. Princes [on the Sabbath], anoint themselves with rose oil on their wounds, since it is their way to do so on ordinary days. R. Simeon says, 'All Israelites are princes'. (*m. Shab.* 14.4; see also *t. Shab.* 12.14)

In Mk 3.1–6 and parallels, Jesus extended the principle of saving life overruling the Sabbath to include his healings. Here Jesus heals a man with a 'withered hand' and defends his actions against Pharisees with the classic argument of saving life: 'Is it lawful to do good or to do harm on the Sabbath, to save life or to kill?'(Mk 3.4). According to Mark, the Pharisees really do not like this interpretation, so much so that they are reported to have sought ways to kill him (Mk 3.6).

Of course, the dispute in Mk 3.1–6 can be read as part of a broader dispute between Jesus and his opponents (and it does follow directly on from another Sabbath dispute over plucking grain) rather than simply just a dispute over healing alone.

The extension of the principle that saving life overrules the Sabbath to include healings is found in stories particular to Luke. In Lk. 13.10–17 Jesus heals a woman who was unable to stand upright for 18 years. The synagogue leader takes the position that such curing is not allowed on the Sabbath while Jesus interprets the releasing of the woman from what he sees as the bondage of Satan an acceptable act by reference to another halakic argument: 'Does not each of you on the Sabbath untie his ox or his donkey from the manger, and lead it away to give it water?' (Lk. 13.15). This reference to untying animals and leading them to water assumes a position which was held by legal interpreters from different perspectives. While there were rabbinic discussions about the tying and untying of different knots on the Sabbath (m. *Shab.* 7.2; 15.1), the various positions relating to cattle going out on the Sabbath is recorded in some detail (*m. Shab.* 5.1–4; *m. 'Erub.* 2.1–4). In such passages we get mention or assumption of the reference to the Sabbath limit, which is mentioned elsewhere in *'Erubin* (4.5), and is 2000 cubits, approximately the equivalent of 1000 yards or 915 metres.[3] Presumably there was a non-exceeding of a Sabbath limit assumed in the dispute in a cornfield over the plucking of the grain in Mk 2.23–28. Here we might also note that even the stricter views from the Dead Sea Scrolls provide scope for cattle within the Sabbath limit: 'No-one should go after an animal to pasture it outside his city, except for two-thousand cubits' (CD 11.5–6).

With these texts in mind, the logic of the argument given by the Lukan Jesus in Lk. 13.15 is to have a general point of agreement on the issue of leading out cattle on the Sabbath and then claim that if this can be agreed upon then should not the release of the woman be celebrated? Unfortunately, we are not given the response of the synagogue leader!

In contrast, Luke claims that scribes and Pharisees had no answer to a related argument given by Jesus when he healed a man with 'dropsy' (Lk. 14.1–6): 'If one of you has a child or an ox that has fallen into a well, will you not immediately pull it out on a Sabbath day?' (Lk. 14.6). While this was, as we have seen, a position which might not have easily been agreed with the writers of CD, it does assume a position with which Pharisees would have agreed. Here we are back in the realm of saving life overruling the Sabbath and how Jesus is presented as seeing his healings as a development of this principle.

PENALTIES FOR SABBATH-BREAKING

According to biblical Law, the punishment for breaking the Sabbath commandment was, in theory, death. Exodus is explicit: 'For six days shall work be done, but on the seventh day you shall have a holy Sabbath of solemn rest to the Lord; whoever does any work on it shall be put to death' (Exod. 35.2). In Num. 15.32–36 a man was stoned to death for gathering sticks on the Sabbath. *Jub.* 2.25–27 also endorses the death penalty for breaking the Sabbath, leaving no room for ambiguity: '. . . let them guard this day . . . and not do any work therein . . . Anyone who pollutes it let him surely die. And anyone who will do any work therein, let him surely die forever so that the children of Israel might guard this day throughout their generations and not be uprooted from the land . . .' Despite such warnings, however, there is no evidence whatsoever of people being put to death for breaking the Sabbath and the difficulty of undertaking such an act might be echoed in Mk 3.6, 'The Pharisees went out and immediately conspired with the Herodians against him, how to destroy him'. In addition to the legal difficulties of putting some to death for such matters, a possible reason why no one appears to have been put to death is that too many Jews were not observing the Sabbath in ways deemed correct and so many people would have had to have been put to death. Perhaps destitute Jews and Jewish slaves had little choice but to work on the Sabbath. Journeying on the Sabbath is not allowed and would potentially have kept at least some Jews from serving in armies (cf. *Ant.* 13.251–252). Josephus writes about dismissals of 'those Jews who were Roman citizens, and were wont to observe the rites of the Jewish religion, on account of their religion' (*Ant.* 14.237). Notice, however, the qualification of not simply Jews who were Roman citizens but also those prepared to follow their practices. Presumably this implies that there were Jews who did, for instance, serve in the armies and were not wont to observe their religious duties so strictly.

Even the strictest group in Second Temple Judaism – those responsible for the Dead Sea Scrolls – decided to go for imprisonment and appear to directly contradict the biblical commandment:

> But everyone who goes astray, defiling the Sabbath and the festivals, shall not be executed, for it is the task of men to guard him; and if he is cured of it, they shall guard him for seven years and afterwards he may enter the assembly . . . (CD 12.3–6)

In rabbinic literature we get the view of deliberate and unintentional Sabbath violations with further technicalities: 'He who profanes the Sabbath – in regard to a matter, on account of the deliberate doing of which they are liable to extirpation, and on account of the inadvertent doing of which they are liable to a sin offering' (*m. Sanh.* 7.8). This is further developed in the Jerusalem Talmud where the idea of giving warning is suggested. Notice here that, along with the distinction between advertent and inadvertent, warning is required making it increasingly more difficult to shift towards the death penalty. Moreover, the first warning was presumably designed to encourage observance. The warning may even have been present in the first century and underlying Mark's recording of Sabbath disputes. If we read Mk 2.23–3.6 as a continuous whole (and remember there were no chapter and verse divisions in the earliest versions of the New Testament) we can observe that from the perspective of Jesus' opponents (though not necessarily from the perspective of Jesus himself) Jesus endorses the deliberate breaking and engages in the deliberate breaking of the Sabbath prohibition of 'work'. This ends in Jesus' opponents conspiring to kill him (Mk 3.6) and notice Mk 3.2: 'They watched him to see whether he would cure him on the Sabbath so that they might accuse him'.[4]

CONCLUDING REMARKS

The Sabbath, the day of rest, was the sixth day and lasted from Friday evening to Saturday evening and was seen as God's gift to Israel. According to biblical Law, the Sabbath should be a day of rest for all of society, including animals, and figures such as Philo interpreted this to mean the whole of creation. The observance of the Sabbath became particularly associated with Jews in the ancient world and attracted both non-Jewish interest and non-Jewish scorn. Much effort was devoted to defining precisely what 'work' might be. Biblical Law only gives a handful of examples and this led to broader defini-tions, including the famous rabbinic 39 prohibitions. Details were, as ever, disputed: from whether it was acceptable to merge courtyards to overcome problems of carrying food from one household to another to whether it was acceptable to fight on the Sabbath, from whether it was acceptable to pick fruit from the ground to spreading nets in advance of the Sabbath to catch animals, birds or fish. There were also exemptions from the Sabbath rest, such as priestly work. However, the most famous exemption is the principle of saving life overruling the Sabbath. More practically, it seems as if there was an avoidance of the death penalty for breaking the Sabbath with solutions ranging from seven-year imprisonment to warnings and distinctions made between intentional and unintentional actions. The New Testament shows a range of views on Sabbath observance. Synoptic Gospel tradition fits neatly into the range of Jewish views outlined here in that they are fairly typical debating of the details. John's Gospel, however, appears to endorse carrying a burden on

Sabbath which is, more or less, directly against biblical Law. This sort of attitude is echoed in Paul's letters where at least some people associated with the Christian movement were not observing Sabbath at all.

CHAPTER 3

PURITY AND FOOD

INTRODUCTION: IMPURITY

Issues relating to pure and impure (or clean and unclean) are arguably the most complex in Jewish Law. In the most basic terms we can say that impurity (or uncleanness) stands in contrast to purity (or cleanness). Lev. 10.10 gives further help: 'You are to distinguish between the holy and the common, the unclean and the clean'. Quite what impurity might be is not entirely clear but some definition as general as the following might help: impurity is a kind of unseen contamination.[1] The laws of purity and impurity are explained in the biblical Law, especially in Leviticus 11–15. Many purity laws are associated with the Temple and the priesthood. This is significant because God was said to dwell in the Temple and so the closer to the Temple a believer was, the more concern for purity laws they must have. It may be the case that priests do not necessarily have to have a blanket avoidance of corpse impurity when not working in the Temple. As Leviticus put it . . .

> The Lord said to Moses: Speak to the priests, the sons of Aaron, and say to them: No one shall defile himself for a dead person among his relatives/people, except for his nearest kin: his mother, his father, his son, his daughter, his brother; likewise, for a virgin sister, close to him because she has had no husband, he may defile himself for her. (Lev. 21.1–3)

45

While God might not like impurity, it was accepted that people will become impure and so regulations were in place to make sure people could become pure again. There were a number of different ways of contracting impurity and a number of ways to become pure again. In some cases, this would involve the most defiling of all impurities: corpse impurity. According to biblical Law, removal of corpse impurity included the uses of the ashes of a red heifer and water of cleansing for sprinkling (Numbers 19). Compare the summary given by Philo:

> And again, in the case of persons who have gone into the house in which any one has died, the law enjoins that no one shall touch them until they have both washed their bodies and also the garments in which they were clothed, and, in a word, it looks upon all the furniture and all the vessels, and everything which is in the house, as unclean and polluted. (*Spec. Leg.* 3.206)

A potentially important passage for the New Testament involves the case of anyone who sits on an object upon which a man with a 'discharge' has sat, has to wash their clothing, immerse themselves, and wait until sunset to become clean again (Lev. 15.4–6). Jesus' contact with the woman with a 12-year bleeding problem in Mk 5.25–34 could have involved issues of impurity and the transmission of impurity as she is healed by touching Jesus' cloak. Leviticus 15.19–24, 25–27 says that if someone comes into contact with a woman with a regular discharge they are impure until the evening and if someone comes into contact with something upon which such a woman sits or lies he 'shall wash his clothes, and bathe in water, and be unclean until the evening' (Lev. 15.19–24) and anyone who comes into contact with anything a woman with a discharge of blood for many days, not during her usual time, sits upon 'shall wash his clothes, and bathe in water, and be unclean until the evening' (Lev. 15.25–27).

The case of what is often called 'leprosy' involves something else. For a start we need to qualify the term 'leprosy' because it is not the equivalent of what we now call 'leprosy' as it is clear from the biblical texts that clothes and houses, as well as people, could get 'leprosy' (Leviticus 13–14). Whoever got this 'infection', or whatever it might be, has to shout 'unclean, unclean' and live outside settled society until the infection has gone (Lev. 13.45–46). If the infection goes, or when they are clean, they are to be inspected by a priest and the priest will declare them clean, accompanied by a lengthy sacrificial procedure involving, among other things, birds and lambs, along with, among other things, shaving and immersion by the one cured. We can see the brief outline of this procedure in Mk 1.40–45. The infected man is *deemed* clean after Jesus heals him and then is sent to the priest to be officially *declared* clean:

> A leper came to him begging him, and kneeling he said to him, 'If you choose, you can make me clean'. And moved with compassion, He stretched out His hand, and touched him, and said to him, 'I am willing; be cleansed'. Immediately the leprosy left him, and he was made . . . 'See that you say nothing to anyone; but go, show yourself to the priest, and offer for your cleansing what Moses commanded, as a testimony to them'. (Mk 1.40–42, 44)

By the first century, there was a range of expansions and interpretations of these purity laws to encompass much of everyday life. However, the role of contracting impurity in the case of an abandoned corpse was up for debate. Compare the following passage:

> A high priest and a Nazir do not contract corpse uncleanness on account of [burying even] their close relatives. But they do contract corpse uncleanness on account of a neglected corpse. [If] they were going along the way and found a neglected corpse – R. Eliezer says, 'Let a high priest contract corpse uncleanness, but let a Nazir not contract corpse uncleanness'. And the Sages say, 'Let a Nazir contract corpse uncleanness, but let a high priest not contract corpse uncleanness'. (*m. Nazir* 7.1)

Some have even argued, Jesus' position according to Luke's telling of the parable of the Good Samaritan (Lk. 10.25–37) would have Jesus closer to the position of Rabbi Eliezer while the character of the Priest (Levites were not prohibited in biblical Law from contracting corpse impurity) was more closely aligned with the position of the Sages, though this could be academic as the idea that the Lukan passage even concerns issues of purity and impurity has been vigorously disputed. We should also qualify this by pointing out that the Mishnah talks more specifically of the *High Priest* and not an ordinary priest of the sort we find in the parable of the Good Samaritan.

There has been some, often fierce, debate over whether this expansion of purity laws was a form of people trying to behave as often as possible like priests serving in Temple, and much depends on how literally we take the language of purity associated with the priesthood (and how much emphasis is placed on *like* in '*like* priests serving in the Temple'). A seemingly extreme version of this view would be that the whole land ought to be treated as if it were just as pure and holy as the Temple and some have attributed this view to the Pharisees. On the other hand, critics of this view have argued that it is impossible for people to behave like priests in the Temple when outside the Temple. It might be easy enough for a priest to avoid corpses and menstruating women when working in the Temple but would this have been so easy in everyday life? Moreover, some of the purity laws which interested people at the time of Jesus were not necessarily priestly, such as those relating to sex and menstruating women. However, if we do not take the language of behaving like a priest too strongly and accept that certain people, including certain Pharisees, dedicated to purity outside the Temple were perhaps imitating priests to some extent then we might be on to something.[2]

A related issue and notable development of the purity laws is the thinking and practice of the Essenes, who clearly saw their community in priestly terms and strictly maintained a state of purity as often as possible. Compare the following description from Josephus:

. . . they assemble themselves together again into one place; and when they have clothed themselves in white veils, they then bathe their bodies in cold water. And after this purification is over, they all meet together in an apartment of their own, into which it is not permitted to any of another sect to enter; while they go, after a pure manner, into the dining room, as into a certain holy temple . . . but a priest says grace before the meal; and it is unlawful for anyone to taste of the food before grace is said. The same priest, when he has dined, says grace again after the meal; and when they begin, and when they end, they praise God, as he that bestows their food upon them; after which they lay aside their [white] garments, and betake themselves to their labours again till the evening . . . Now after the time of their preparatory trial is over, they are divided into four classes; and so far are the juniors inferior to the seniors, that if the seniors should be touched by the juniors, they must wash themselves as if they had intermixed themselves with the company of a foreigner. (*War* 2.129–131, 150)

As we have seen in passing, the dominant explanation for the question of who wrote the Dead Sea Scrolls is that they were Essenes. One of the reasons for this is that there appears to be a very similar role on issues of purity and the purity of the community in the Scrolls where meals were eaten in a state of purity. Whatever explanation we choose for the authorship of the Scrolls, the idea of a pure priestly community is clear enough, most strikingly in the Community Rule (1QS):

This is the rule for the men of the community . . . They should keep apart from the congregation of the men of justice in order to constitute a Community in law and possessions, and acquiesce to the authority of the sons of Zadok, the priests who safeguard the covenant . . . He shall swear a binding oath to revert to the Law of Moses, according to all that he commanded, with whole heart and whole soul, in compliance with all that has been revealed of it to the sons of Zadok, the priests who keep the covenant and interpret his will . . . He should not go into the waters to share in the pure food of the men of holiness, for one is not cleansed unless one turns away from one's wickedness, for he is unclean among all the transgressors of his word . . . (1QS 5.1–2, 8–9, 13, 14)

Archaeological evidence has shown that immersion pools for the removal of impurity were present throughout first century Palestine. The importance of immersion pools (sg. *miqweh*; pl. *miqwaoth*) is grounded in biblical Law. We have already mentioned cases in Leviticus 15 of people having to immerse themselves and wait until sunset. The water should be, according to Leviticus 15, 'fresh water' (Lev. 15.13). According to Leviticus 11, 'a spring or a cistern holding water shall be clean' (Lev. 11.36). In addition to people, a variety of utensils (*kelim*) had to be immersed in precise cases (Lev. 11.32–33; 15.12) and we will return to these issues shortly.

The concern for immersion was expanded and interpreted in early Judaism and a whole rabbinic tractate, *Miqwa'oth*, is dedicated to the very issue. It also seems as if certain Jews were concerned to eat their ordinary food in a state of purity and immerse themselves. There is a possible hint of this in the book of Judith:

> . . . and sent this message to Holofernes: 'Let my lord now give orders to allow your servant to go out and pray'. So Holofernes commanded his guards not to hinder her. She remained in the camp three days. She went out each night to the valley of Bethulia, and bathed at the spring in the camp. After bathing, she prayed the Lord God of Israel to direct her way for the triumph of his people. Then she returned purified and stayed in the tent until she ate her food toward evening. On the fourth day Holofernes held a banquet for his personal attendants only, and did not invite any of his officers. (Judith 12.6–10)

In Mark's Gospel, we read, according to some translations, 'they do not eat anything from the market unless they wash it'. However, an alternative translation is 'when they come from the market-place, they do not eat unless they immerse themselves'. Grammatically, by far the best way to translate this verse is in terms of bodily immersion but there is an additional, but no less important, cultural argument: there are numerous examples of bodily immersion from earliest Judaism and, as far as I am aware, there are no examples of washing food in the context of hand-washing. The bringing together of washing hands and immersion before a bodily meal and attributing it to a Pharisaic (and indeed broader) practice is reflected in rabbinic literature. This is a complex area of study so it is worth discussing both washing hands and bodily immersion separately before seeing how they are both connected with eating.

WASHING HANDS

Washing hands before ordinary food is documented in rabbinic literature in the sense that it is an assumed practice even if the details are disputed. Put quite simply in one passage from the Mishnah, 'They wash the hands for unconsecrated food . . .' (*m. Hag.* 2.5). But why wash hands before an ordinary meal for reason other than basic hygiene? Here we need to move into arguably the most complex area of all: the transmission of impurity from unwashed hands to food to eater.[3]

The transmission of impurity according to rabbinic literature is based on a graded system of impurity. A 'father of impurity' is a scriptural source of impurity, such as a menstruating woman or a 'leper', and can render something impure in the first degree (or first remove from the scriptural source). Something rendered impure in the first degree can then render something impure in the second degree (or second remove from the scriptural source) and something in the second degree can then render something else impure in the third degree and, finally, something impure in the third degree can then render something impure in the fourth degree. Certain objects can only be susceptible to certain degrees of impurity. Typically, only things associated with the priesthood and Temple were susceptible to third and fourth degree impurity due to their particularly holy nature. Hands were conventionally susceptible to impurity in the second degree while food was only able to be made unclean by a 'father of impurity' or something of first degree impurity:

> He who pokes his hands into a house afflicted with *nega* ('leprosy') – 'his hands are in the first remove of uncleanness,' the words of R. Aqiba. And sages say, 'His hands are in the second remove of uncleanness'. Whoever imparts uncleanness to clothing, when in contact [with them] imparts uncleanness to the hands – 'So that they are in the first remove of uncleanness'. Said they to R. Aqiba, 'When do we find that the hands are in the first remove of uncleanness under any circumstances whatsoever?' He said to them, 'And how is it possible for them to be in the first remove of uncleanness without his body's [being] made unclean, outside of the present case?'
>
> 'Food and utensils which have been made unclean by liquids impart uncleanness to the hands so that they are in the second remove of uncleanness', the words of R. Joshua.
>
> And the sages say, 'That which is made unclean by a Father of Uncleanness imparts uncleanness to the hands. [That which has been made unclean] by an Offspring of Uncleanness does not impart uncleanness to the hands'. (*m. Yad.* 3.1)
>
> . . . the third remove is clean for unconsecrated food . . . (*m. T. Yom* 4.1, 3)

In terms of hand-washing before ordinary meals, it would seem as if we have a problem with this logic because impure hands (assumed to be second degree impure) cannot make food impure. Thus, impure hands by themselves cannot make food impure and so, according to this logic, why bother washing hands if it makes no difference? Here liquids become extremely important in the transmission of impurity.

The importance of liquids in the transmission of impurity has a biblical basis. In Lev. 11.32–34, 38 we read:

> And anything upon which any of them falls when they are dead shall be unclean, whether an article of wood or cloth or skin or sacking, any article that is used for any purpose; it shall be dipped into water, and it shall be unclean until the evening, and then it shall be clean. And if any of them falls into any earthen vessel, all that is in it shall be unclean, and you shall break the vessel. Any food that could be eaten shall be unclean if water from any such vessel comes upon it; and any liquid that could be drunk shall be unclean if it was in any such vessel . . . but if water is put on the seed and any part of their carcass falls on it, it is unclean for you.

The concept of water 'put on' was developed further by the time of rabbinic literature, most notably in the rabbinic tractate *Makshirin*. In rabbinic literature it becomes clear that liquids have an intensifying function in the transmission of impurity. In a famous and much discussed passage (and one to which we will return), attributed to the first century houses of Hillel and Shammai, the Mishnah records that the House of Shammai say, 'They wash the hands then mix the cup' whereas the House of Hillel say, 'They mix the cup then wash the hands' (*m. Ber.* 8.2). The role of liquids underlies the dispute in this passage and this is made explicit in the version in the Tosefta where the House of Shammai's order of washing hands then mixing the cup is explained: 'lest liquids on the outer surface of the cup become impure through contact with hands and in turn render the cup impure' (*t. Ber.* 5.26).

In terms of hands and food, this meant that something of second degree impurity, such as impure hands, could pass on impurity to ordinary food: 'this one [food] says [to liquid], The things which made you unclean could not have made me unclean but you have made me unclean' (*m. Parah* 8.7; cf. *m. Zab.* 5.12; *m. Hul.* 2.5; *b. Hul.* 33a).

Rabbinic literature also gives us a range of liquids which defile such as dew, water, wine, oil, blood, milk and honey (*m. Maksh.* 6.4), all of which are directly relevant to the meal table. Rabbinic literature gives practical examples of the transmission of impurity from hands to food via a liquid. Compare, for instance, the following: 'He who slaughters a beast, a wild animal, or fowl, from which blood did not exude – they are valid. And they are eaten with dirty hands, because they have not been made susceptible to uncleanness by blood' (*m. Hul.* 2.5). This involves the slaughtering of wild animals, and thus ordinary, non-priestly, food, and the blood acts as a conductor for impurity. If there is no blood, the animal may be eaten with impure hands because the impurity cannot pass from hands to the food without a liquid.

As ever, we should note that there were different views on matters relating to the washing of hands and the transmission of impurity. While there were some who did not view hand-washing in itself as the highest of priorities (*t. Ber.* 5.13), there were rabbis who (controversially) believed food could become impure in the third degree: 'R. Aqiba . . . "Thus has Scripture taught concerning a loaf of bread unclean in the second remove, that it imparts uncleanness in the third remove [to a loaf of bread with which it comes into contact]"' (*m. Sotah* 5.3). Others, notably in later in the rabbinic period, claimed a lack of sufficient biblical basis such as the following from the Babylonian Talmud: 'the washing of hands for secular food is not from the Torah' (*b. Ber.* 52b). One solution to such a potential problem is found in the thinking of Rab Judah who argued that the washing of hands was instituted by Solomon (*b. Shab.* 14b; cf. *b. 'Erub.* 21b). According to R. Idi b. Abin in the name of R. Isaac b. Ashian washing hands before non-priestly food was more a useful practice for handling priestly food (*b. Hullin* 105a). Others, though, were more serious about washing hands:

Our Rabbis taught: R. Aqiba was once confined in a prison-house and R. Joshua the grits maker was attending on him. Every day, a certain quantity of water was brought in to him. On one occasion he [R. Joshua] was met by the prison keeper who said to him, 'Your water to-day is rather much; do you perhaps require it for undermining the prison?' He poured out a half of it and handed to him the other half. When he [R. Joshua] came to R. Aqiba the latter said to him, 'Joshua, do you not know that I am an old man and my life depends on yours?' When the latter told him all that had happened [R. Aqiba] said to him, 'Give me some water to wash my hands'. 'It will not suffice for drinking', the other complained, 'will it suffice for washing your hands?' 'What can I do', the former replied, 'when for [neglecting] the words of them [the Rabbis] one deserves death? It is better that I myself should die than that I should transgress against the opinion of my colleagues [who ordained the washing of hands before meals]. It was related that he tasted nothing until the other had brought him water wherewith to wash his hands. When the Sages heard of this incident they remarked, 'If he was so [scrupulous] in his old age how much more must he have been so in his youth; and if he so [behaved] in a prison-house how much more [must he have behaved in such a manner] when not in a prison-house'. (b. 'Erub. 21b)

On the role of liquids, it is worth pointing out that the idea of a liquid conducting impurity was developed in early Judaism by the time of the New Testament texts. The Dead Sea Scrolls, for instance, applied the laws of liquids to different situations and this is seen in 4Q284a and 4Q274 (frag. 3), the 4QTohorot texts. All crops were susceptible to impurity if they became wet. This was even more so in the case of foodstuffs such as grapes which contain liquid that can easily come to the surface and thus conduct impurity. This meant that even those who harvested had to harvest the crops in a state of purity. This would have been very important for the Dead Sea Scrolls group because the communal meals at Qumran were eaten in a state of purity.

Another important text from Qumran which discusses the impurity of liquids is 4QMMT[a] (=4Q394) frag. 8, col. IV 5–7, where we read that in no circumstances should liquids be regarded as preventing impurity: '. . . also concerning liquid streams: we say that in these there is no [pu]rity, and also that liquid streams cannot separate impure [from] pure, because the liquid of the liquid streams and their vessels is alike, the same liquid'. Here it appears to be the case that if liquid was poured from an impure vessel into a pure vessel the pure vessel becomes impure because of the liquid conducting impurity. Indeed, it implies that if liquid was poured from a pure vessel into an impure vessel, all would become unclean due to the impurity being conducted by water. This sort of position appears to have been rejected by the Pharisees and accepted by the 'Sadducees' according to the Mishnah: 'Say Sadducees: "We complain against you, Pharisees. For you declare clean an unbroken stream of liquids"' (*m. Yad.* 4.7). Oil was a liquid which could also be deemed to transmit impurity. In the Dead Sea Scrolls this is certainly the case with a corpse. According to CD 12.15–17, '. . . And all the wood and the stones and the dust which are defiled by man's impurity, while with stains of oil in them, in accordance with their uncleanness will make whoever touches them impure . . .'

WASHING HANDS AND THE *TEBUL YOM*

One question we might ask is this: precisely what is being prevented from becoming impure by washing hands? John Poirier has argued that passages such as *b. Ber.* 28a, and the idea of a person whose 'insides are not as their outsides', concern an early idea associated with those who disagreed with Pharisees, namely those people who did not keep their insides pure through the washing of hands while keeping their outsides pure through immersion.[4] We may well have a first century example of this from Mark 7. Mark 7.1–23 is framed in terms of a dispute over hand washing (Mk 7.1–5) and Jesus' response and rejection of such a view of impurity is that, there is nothing outside a person that by going in can defile, but the things that come out are what defile' (Mk 7.15). Mark also adds that Pharisees immerse themselves in this context (Mk 7.3) and this too reflects issues relating to hand-washing and, in particularly, the issue of the *tebul yom*. The *tebul yom* is simply someone who has immersed that day and is waiting for sunset to be deemed pure again, something we have already seen in passing with reference to Leviticus 15. The status of the *tebul yom* was a debateable issue because, according to rabbinic literature, the *tebul yom* could do many, though certainly not all, things a pure person could do.

In rabbinic literature, the idea of the *tebul yom* in relation to the washing of hands is, as in Mk 7.1–5, a significant issue. Like hands, a *tebul yom* is assumed second degree impure. However, *unlike* hands, a *tebul yom* could not render a liquid impure, despite both being second degree impure. This might seem to make the process of hand washing unnecessary if a person had immersed first, as in Mk 7.3, because there should be no problem in making things impure, should there not? There was, however, an important qualification: while the whole body could be immersed, hands were deemed to be able to become impure separately and in distinction from the rest of the body and so hands still had to be washed to prevent the transmission of impurity. Compare the following:

> A cooking pot which is full of liquids, and which a *tebul yom* touched – if it was liquid of heave offering, the liquids are unfit, but the pot is clean. And if it was liquid of unconsecrated, all is clean. And if his hands were dirty, all is unclean. This rule is more stringent in the case of hands than in the case of the *tebul yom*. And more stringent is the rule pertaining to the *tebul yom* than pertaining to hands: For a matter of doubt in connection with the *tebul yom* spoils heave offering, but as to hands, a matter of doubt concerning them is deemed to be clean. (*m. T. Yom* 2.2)

This seems to be the sort of logic Mark attributes to the dispute between Jesus and the Pharisees. According to Mark, the Pharisees immerse on return from the marketplace but still insist on washing their hands before an ordinary meal.

IMMERSION AND WIPING OF UTENSILS

Mark mentions various other details relating, contextually at least, to the washing of hands, such as: 'the washing of cups, pots, and bronze kettles [and beds]' (Mk 7.4). These practices appear to have been grounded in biblical law but expanded and interpreted in Second Temple Judaism. We have already seen the context of the biblical precedent for such laws in Lev. 11.30–33 and we can add another: 'Any earthen vessel that one with the discharge touches shall be broken; and every vessel of wood shall be rinsed in water' (Lev. 15.12). This is expanded more generally in the numerous passages dealing with the uncleanness of wood in the Mishnah such as the following: 'Utensils of wood, leather, bone, or glass that are flat are not suscep-tible to uncleanness. If they form a receptacle they are susceptible' (*m. Kelim* 15.1). With Lev. 11.30–33 in mind, the practice of immers-ing other kinds of utensils was developed in rabbinic literature. There are more general statements in rabbinic literature concerning the immersion of vessels such as the following: 'R. Meir says: Vessels may be immersed in the water but not in the mud. R. Joshua says: Either in the water or in the mud . . . ' (*m. Miqw.* 3.10). Like the bronze kettle of Mk 7.4, *m. Kelim* 11.1 indicates that metal objects are indeed susceptible: 'Utensils of metal are susceptible to unclean-ness whether they are flat or whether they form a receptacle . . .' (m. *Kelim* 11.1).

One material that Mark would *not* have been referring to was earthenware because earthenware had to be smashed if impure (Lev. 11.33). Another material probably not implied by Mark because, according to the Mishnah, for instance, stone was not necessarily susceptible to impurity: 'an oven made of stone or metal is clean . . . A stove made of stone or of metal is clean . . . These utensils afford protection with a tightly stopped-up cover: vessels [made] . . . of stone . . . ' (*m. Kelim* 5.11; 10.1). In fact, a key archaeological find to support a widespread dedication to purity outside the Temple is stone vessels. Throughout the whole of Palestine/Israel stone vessels have been found. For some scholars this suggests that at least some people were concerned with having meals in a state of purity in different geographical areas and, given that the ruling on stone vessels is found in rabbinic literature and given the connections between the Pharisees and the rabbis, that this practice can probably can be said to have been a Pharisaic concern in the first century.

One particular utensil mentioned in some manuscripts of Mark's Gospel, and which has caused confusion among ancient copyists and modern scholars alike, is the mention of the immersion of 'beds' or, better, 'dining couches' (Mk 7.4). The confusion is typically over the impossibility of the given interpreter imagining people to have done such things and it has even been known for scholars to claim Mark invented the practice. However, it is quite clear that certain practices were discussed in rabbinic literature as in the following passages:

[If] one immersed the bed/dining couch therein, even though its legs sink down into thick mud – it is clean, because the water touched them before [the mud did]. (*m. Miqw*. 7.7)

He who unties the bed/dining couch to immerse it . . . (*m. Kelim* 19.1)

While some have argued that this could be a reference to the 'beds' of Leviticus 15 which become impure, this is probably not the case. In addition to the word for 'bed' in Leviticus 15 not typically having the connotations of 'dining couches' (in contrast to Mark 7 and the above passages from the Mishnah), there is no mention of immersion for the 'beds' of Leviticus 15. Instead, the 'beds' of Mark 7 and the Mishnah passages are part of the same general laws of 'utensils' found in Lev. 11.32 and 15.12.[5]

Why immerse all these kinds of utensils and furniture? Again, the issue involves the transmission of impurity and we have a notable discussion of a directly related issue in a passage recorded in Matthew (and Luke):[6]

Woe to you, scribes and Pharisees, hypocrites! For you clean the outside of the cup and of the plate, but inside they are full of greed and self-indulgence. You blind Pharisee! First clean the inside of the cup [and of the plate], so that the outside also may become clean. (Mt. 23.25–26; see also Lk. 11.39–41)

The cleansing of cups and the idea of insides and outsides of cups are further complex purity issues discussed in rabbinic literature. We have already seen m. Ber. 8.2: 'The House of Shammai say, "They wash the hands and then mix the cup [of wine]". But the House of Hillel say, "They mix the cup and then wash the hands"' as well as the important interpretation of this dispute in the Tosefta:

The House of Shammai say, They wash the hands then mix the cup – lest liquids on the outer surface of the cup become impure through contact with hands and in turn render the cup impure. The House of Hillel say, The outer surface of the cup is always deemed impure. (t. Ber. 5.26)

The other most prominent text in discussions of washing cups is m. Kelim 25 where the distinction between the inside and outside of certain things is made bluntly at the beginning: 'All utensils have outsides and an inside' (m. Kelim 25.1). The idea of a third part of utensils is also present but not without controversy, firstly between R. Tarfon and R. Aqiba and then R. Meir and R. Yose. The passage is difficult and ought to be quoted at length: (m. Kelim 25.7a)

All utensils have outer parts and an inner part, and they [further] have a part by which they are held. R. Tarfon says, [This distinction in the outer parts applies only] to a large wooden trough. Aqiba says, To cups. R. Meir says, To the unclean and the clean hands. Said R. Yose, They have spoken only concerning clean hands alone. How so? [If] one's hands were clean, and the outer parts of the cup were unclean, [and] one took [the cup] with its holding part, he need not worry lest his hands be made unclean on the outer parts of the cup. [If] one was drinking from a cup, the outer parts of which are unclean, one does not worry lest the liquid which is in his mouth be made unclean on the outer parts of the cup and go and render the [whole] cup unclean. A kettle [unclean on the outside] which is boiling – one does not worry lest the liquids go forth from it and touch its outer parts and go back to the inside [and make it unclean]. (*m. Kelim* 25.7–8)

The discussion between the houses of Shammai and Hillel previously mentioned accord with the two different positions of R. Meir and R. Yose in this passage from *Kelim*. As R. Biban in the name of R. Yohanan put it according to the Palestinian Talmud, 'The opinion of the House of Shammai accords with the view of R. Yose, and the opinion of the House of Hillel accords with the view of R. Meir' (*y. Ber.* 8.2).

The position of Yose and the House of Shammai is this: '[If] one's hands were clean, and the outer parts of the cup were unclean, [and] one took [the cup] with its holding part, he need not worry lest his hands be made unclean on the outer parts of the cup' (*m. Kelim* 25.8). But, as the House of Shammai put it, this position cannot apply to impure hands 'lest liquids on the outer surface of the cup become impure through contact with hands and in turn render the cup impure' (*t. Ber.* 5.26).

The position of Meir and the House of Hillel is this: '[If] one's hands were clean, and the outer parts of the cup were unclean, [and] one took [the cup] with its holding part, he need not worry lest his hands be made unclean on the outer parts of the cup' (*m. Kelim* 25.8). Where Yose and the House of Shammai first washed the hands, Meir and the House of Hillel do not think the issue of liquids on the outer surface of the cup is relevant and so even impure hands could not make the whole cup impure through contact with the liquid on the outside of the cup.

How can an outside of a cup become clean if we follow Matthew's polemic that Pharisees wash the outside of the cup? This idea of washing the outside of the cup can get even more confusing because if utensils such as cups became impure then, as we have seen, the simple solution was to immerse them. But when cups are immersed then the whole cup is obviously immersed, not simply the outside (cf. *m. Miqw.* 5.6; 6.2, 5–6). However, there were outer parts of the cup (the handle, the rim, the handles etc) which were not immersed but wiped according to *Kelim*:

> Bases of utensils, and their rims, and their hangers, and the handles of utensils which hold [something = which have a receptacle], on which fell [unclean] liquids – *one dries them, and they are clean* . . . A utensil, the outer parts of which have been made unclean with liquids – the outer parts are unclean. Its inside, its rims, hangers, and handles are clean. [If] its inside is made unclean, the whole is unclean. (*m. Kelim* 25.6)

It may well be, then, that this wiping of certain outside parts of cups is reflected in the polemic recorded more generally in Mt. 23.25–26.

LIQUIDS, UTENSILS AND THE PEOPLE OF THE LAND

Related divergent viewpoints on purity occur in rabbinic literature and particularly with reference to the 'people of the land', sometimes seen as an important background to gospel passages on purity. The 'people of the land' are best understood as a religious category rather than a class based category (e.g. 'the poor'): this group could include people from agricultural workers to people who owned property and slaves (e.g. *t. Dem.* 3.5; *t. Abod. Zar.* 3.9) and were defined in terms of their observance of rabbinic or Pharisaic or *haberim* tithing and/or purity laws (*t. Abod. Zar.* 3.10; *b. Ber.* 43b; *b. Git.* 61a; *b. Ned.* 90b; *ARN* [A] 41; cf. *m. Hag.* 2.7). The issues are conveniently summarized in the following reflections in the Babylonian Talmud: 'It has been taught, "Who is a person of the land? Anyone who does not eat his secular food in ritual purity." This is the opinion of R. Meir. The Sages, however, said, "Anyone who does not tithe his produce properly."' (*b. Ber.* 47b). We might compare a first century example of an overarching religious categorization covering different class distinctions where Josephus describes the building of Tiberias in Galilee. What reference to the Jesus tradition may already show, people did disagree on how to interpret purity laws. Josephus gives an example in his discussion of the building of the Galilean city of Tiberias by Herod Antipas:

> The new settlers were a promiscuous rabble, no small contingent being Galilean, with such as were drafted from territory subject to him [Herod Antipas] and brought forcibly to the new foundation. Some of these were magistrates. Herod accepted as participants even poor men who were brought in to join the others from any and all places of origin. It was question whether some were even free beyond cavil. These latter he often and in large bodies liberated and benefited imposing the condition that they should not quit the city, by equipping houses at his own expense and adding new gifts of land. For he knew that this settlement was contrary to the law and tradition of the Jews because Tiberias was built on the site of tombs that had been obliterated, of which there were many there. And our law declares that such settlers are unclean for seven days. (*Ant.* 18.36–38)

Willingly or not, people from different parts of the social spectrum were to populate Tiberias and face continual problems of impurity. From Antipas' perspective, any potentially mischievous Pharisees, or anyone else dedicated to purity laws, could presumably be kept at a distance.

More specifically, the 'people of the land' were perceived to be suspect in transmission of impurity. This is assumed in the following example: 'He who gives over his key to a person of the land – the house is clean, for he gave him only [the charge of] guarding the key' (*m. Tohorot* 7.1). Others took another line. According to R. Simeon, 'He who gave a key to a person of the land – the house is unclean' (*t. Tohorot* 8.1). Both cases clearly assume that in some way the person of the land is a problem in relation to keeping pure. Specifics were further debated (*m. Tohorot* 7.2). The Pharisees' interest in the people of the land and purity is recorded in a famous passage of a gradation of purity/impurity moving from the people of the land through to the Temple itself:

> The clothing of a person of the land is in the status of *midras* uncleanness [e.g. one with a discharge] for Pharisees [who eat ordinary food in a state of uncleanness], the clothing of Pharisees is in the status of *midras* uncleanness for those who eat *terumah* [i.e. priests]. The clothing of those who eat heave offering is in the status of *midras* uncleanness for those who eat Holy Things [i.e. officiating priests] etc . . . (*m. Hagigah* 2.7)

Here the impurity of the clothes of a person of the land is compared with the impurity of one with a discharge and connections with scriptural impurity (or fathers of impurity) are found elsewhere in rabbinic literature. They are suspect in relation to utensils: 'He who deposits utensils with a person of the land – they are unclean with corpse uncleanness and unclean with *midras* uncleanness' (*m. Tohorot* 8.2).

The people of the land are also deemed to be careless with liquids which, of course, are extremely important in the transmission of impurity (cf. *t. Abod. Zar.* 4.11) and there are debates over the specifics of what comes under the law of water being 'put on': 'The water which comes up (1) on the snares, (2) on the gins, and (3) on the nets is not under the law, *If water be put*. And if he shook [them to remove the water], it [the water which is detached] is under the law, *If water be put*' (*m. Maksh.* 5.7). The significance of liquids is reinforced in definitions of a *haber* and their strict purity laws in relation to the people of the land. A *haber*, according to the Mishnah, is partly defined by not purchasing wet produce 'which has been rendered susceptible to uncleanness . . . ' (*m. Demai* 2.3), though dry produce is, according to the Palestinian Talmud, allowed because people of the land 'are deemed trustworthy with respect to rendering produce susceptible to impurity' (*y. Demai* 2, 22d).

SUMMARY

Whether the rabbinic debates over the people of the land are a precise context for the gospel disputes is for another discussion. For now, following the spirit of this book, the intention is just to show the developments of debates over purity laws which have thematic links with New Testament texts. We have seen that impurity is a kind of unseen contamination which needs to be avoided especially, but not exclusively, closer to the heart of the Temple the Jewish believer becomes, hence many purity laws associated with Temple and priesthood. Of course, given that impurity could be contracted from, for instance, corpses, sexual intercourse, menstruating women, and people with skin diseases, then it was perhaps inevitable that people would become impure. Indeed, biblical Law gives plenty of instruction for becoming pure again.

The purity laws were developed by certain groups and figures to encompass all of daily life, or at least as much as possible. The group responsible for the Dead Sea Scrolls wrote about eating communal meals in a state of purity. It seems that groups such as the Pharisees were keen to eat their ordinary food in a state of purity. This involved bodily immersion, immersion of various utensils (e.g. cups) and, ultimately, the washing of hands. This practice prevented the transmission of impurity from hands to food (via a liquid) to the eater. The reasoning for this, it seems, was to keep the insides pure. Of course, details were disputed and it looks as if the Jesus of Mark (and Matthew) was among those rejecting the significance of hand-washing before ordinary meals and the transmission of impurity to the insides. The 'people of the land' were also among those with a more lax attitude relating to these expanded purity laws and the role of liquids in the transmission of impurity.

CHAPTER 4

DIVORCE, 'EYE FOR AN EYE' AND OATHS AND VOWS

The three categories of divorce, 'eye for an eye' and oaths/vows are brought together in this chapter because they occur in a much discussed and much misunderstood (at least in terms of Jewish law) section in Matthew's Gospel: the so-called 'antitheses' (Mt. 5.21–48). We may broadly call this 'civil law' in that they are the kinds of legal interpretations which have had an influence on legal systems right up to those in liberal democracies in a way that, say, laws of impurity have not. Indeed, part of the reasoning for this is that these sorts of laws are not flashpoints in earliest Christianity when the issue of the Law arose and are more broadly applicable to human societies. Despite this, however, people still regularly interpret such texts in terms of difference from Judaism and so more details of Jewish Law are required for further insight. We may begin with 'divorce'.

DIVORCE

In many texts, as we will see, divorce is thought to be a 'necessary evil', even if some would provide 'easier' means of divorce than others. Figures such as Jesus and Paul believed that divorce was a bad thing (cf. Mal. 2.13–16; Mk 10.5; 1 Cor. 7.10–16; *m. Git.* 9.10; *b. Git.* 90b). Marriage, so the logic of this sort of argument went, ought to be a very good thing. So Mk 10.6–8, citing Gen. 1.27; 2.24: 'But from the beginning of creation, "God made them male and female."

"For this reason a man shall leave his father and mother and be joined to his wife, and the two shall become one flesh." So they are no longer two, but one flesh'. This sort of view was known elsewhere, with the Genesis texts being central, as in the following example from the Dead Sea Scrolls: 'The builders of the wall . . . are caught twice in fornication: by taking two wives in their lives, even though the principle of creation is "male and female he created them"' (CD 4.21).

If marriage was deemed so important, then perhaps it is no surprise that adultery was, ideally, punishable by death:

> If a man commits adultery with the wife of his neighbour, both the adulterer and the adulteress shall be put to death. (Lev. 20.10)

> If a man is caught lying with the wife of another man, both of them shall die, the man who lay with the woman as well as the woman. So you shall purge the evil from Israel. (Deut. 22.22)

However, as with Sabbath punishments, there is no evidence the death penalty was ever imposed, presumably because far too many people would have to be killed. The closest we get in the first century is the story found in some versions of John's Gospel (Jn 8.1–11) where scribes and Pharisees bring an adulterous woman to Jesus and mention the not indelicate point that the Law commands that such a woman ought to be stoned. They are said to try to catch Jesus out in order to bring a charge against him by asking, 'Now what do you say?' (Jn 8.6). Jesus was said, of course, to give his famous answer about the one without sin casting the first stone but perhaps more significantly for our purposes we have an example where there seems to be an assumption that people were avoiding the Law by not stoning such adulterous people and the test was, presumably, to see how Jesus could answer the question by contradicting the Law. But whatever we make of this story, it remains that this woman does not provide evidence of someone being stoned for adultery.[1]

The foundational biblical text for divorce was Deut. 24.1–4:

Suppose a man enters into marriage with a woman, but she does not please him because he finds something objectionable about her, and so he writes her a certificate of divorce, puts it in her hand and sends her out of his house; she then leaves his house and goes off to become another man's wife. Then suppose the second man dislikes her, writes her a bill of divorce, puts it in her hand and sends her out of his house (or the second man who married her dies); her first husband, who sent her away, is not permitted to take her again to be his wife after she has been defiled; for that would be abhorrent to the LORD, and you shall not bring guilt on the land that the LORD your God is giving you as a possession.

The phrase 'finds something objectionable about her' became one of the foci for debate on issues of divorce. Precisely what constitutes 'something objectionable'? In a notable way to end the Mishnah tractate *Gittin*, two famous interpretations of Deut. 24.1–4 are represented by two major rabbinic traditions, the 'strict' House of Shammai, on the one hand and the not-so-'strict' House of Hillel and R. Aqiba, on the other:

> The House of Shammai say, 'A man should divorce his wife only because he has found grounds for it in unchastity, since it is said, *Because he has found in her indecency in anything* [i.e. something objectionable] (Deut. 24.1)'. And the House of Hillel say, 'Even if she spoiled his dish, since it is said, *Because he has found in her indecency in anything* [i.e. something objectionable]'. R. Aqiba says, 'Even if he found someone else prettier than she, since it is said, *And it shall be if she find no favour in his eyes* (Deut. 24.1)'. (*m. Git.* 9.10; cf. *Sifre* Deut. 269; *y. Sota* 1.2, 16b)

Such concerns over the phrase 'something objectionable' is presumably underlying the question asked by the Pharisees in Matthew's Gospel, 'Is it lawful for a man to divorce his wife for any cause?' (Mt. 19.3). Certainly the 'stricter' idea of a man divorcing his wife for sexually related acts was present by the first century. Markus Bockmuehl has shown that the husband would be required to divorce an adulterous or raped wife because the wife was made unclean.[2] This sort of view is echoed, for instance, in the retelling of the story of Abram and Sarai (Abraham and Sarah) in Egypt. According to Philo, the Egyptian leader wanted to seduce Sarai but God protected her and physically punished him thereby protecting Sarai's chastity and protecting the marriage from violation (*Abr.* 93–8). According to the Genesis Apocryphon from the Dead Sea Scrolls, Abram pleads with God, 'Do justice for me against him and show your mighty arm against him, and against all his house. During this night, may he not be able to defile my wife, separated from me . . .' (1QapGen. 20.15). We can also compare Mt. 1.19 here when Joseph believes Mary has been unfaithful and the text simply assumes Mary will be divorced: 'Joseph, being a righteous man and unwilling to expose her to public disgrace, planned to dismiss her quietly'. Similarly, according to later rabbinic literature it seems as if a husband was to divorce an adulterous wife:

> Aforetimes they did rule: three sorts of women go forth and collect their marriage contract: she who says, 'I am unclean for you' . . . They reverted to rule: so that a woman should not covet someone else and spoil [her relationship with] her husband, but: she who says, 'I am unclean for you', must bring proof for her claim . . . (*m. Ned.* 11.12)

We may also have another New Testament parallel in the case of the woman Jesus meets at the well in John 4. Jesus said to her, 'for you have had five husbands, and the one you have now is not your husband. What you have said is true!' (Jn 4.18). This woman is a Samaritan and thus not Jewish (as John puts it, 'Jews do not share things in common with Samaritans' – Jn 4.9) but Samaritans also have the Pentateuch as a central document and so here we may be dealing with assumed cases of divorce for adultery.

In terms of divorce for adultery, we could follow David Instone-Brewer here and compare Mk 10.5 on the role of Deut. 24.1–4: 'But Jesus said to them, "Because of your hardness of heart he wrote this commandment for you".' Instone-Brewer suggests that the phrase 'hardness of heart' is an echo of scriptural concerns for Israel's 'hardness of heart' that occurs metaphorically in the context of marriage and divorce and the charge that Israel has repeatedly committed 'adultery' by more than fluttering her eyelids at idols and without listening to God. Thus 'divorce' is inevitable (Jer. 3–4, esp. LXX Jer. 4.4).[3]

The Hillel/Aqiba view of divorce for almost anything was also present by the time of the first century. In Matthew's longer version of the divorce passage (Mt. 19.1–12) we can see this. Matthew here and elsewhere (Mt. 5.32) makes qualifications not explicitly present in Mark when he adds his famous 'exception clauses': 'And I say to you, whoever divorces his wife, except for *porneia* (sexual immorality), and marries another commits adultery' (Mt. 19.9). However, even with these exception clauses it is clear that Matthew at least knows of views which find it difficult to accept divorce, even for the reason of *porneia*: 'His disciples said to him, "If such is the case of a man with his wife, it is better not to marry"' to which Jesus replies, 'Not everyone can accept this teaching, but only those to whom it is given' (Mt. 19.10–11). This clearly assumes a situation where men were expecting to divorce wives for a wider range of reasons, perhaps agreeing with the position of the House of Hillel and R. Aqiba. More than 250 years prior to Matthew, Ben Sirah had the following to say about wives and divorce:

I would rather live with a lion and a dragon than live with an evil woman. A woman's wickedness changes her appearance, and darkens her face like that of a bear. Her husband sits among the neighbours, and he cannot help sighing bitterly . . . Dejected mind, gloomy face, and wounded heart come from an evil wife. Drooping hands and weak knees come from the wife who does not make her husband happy . . . *If she does not go as you direct, separate her from yourself* . . . But it is heartache and sorrow when a wife is jealous of a rival, and a tongue-lashing makes it known to all. A bad wife is a chafing yoke; taking hold of her is like grasping a scorpion. A drunken wife arouses great anger; she cannot hide her shame. (Sirach 25.16–18, 23, 26; 26.6–8 [my italics])

While these sentiments may not provide quite as 'easy' means to divorce, clearly they are along the same lines as those of Hillel, Aqiba and certain figures linked with Matthew's Gospel in that a women is to be divorced if she does not please her husband in very general terms.

One of the functions of the 'stricter' view of divorce may have been an attempt to prevent people from divorcing simply for the sake of remarriage, something which might have been seen in arguments favouring divorce for the wife burning supper or a prettier wife being found. The critique of divorce for the sake of remarriage is certainly emphasized, in their own different ways, in the different Gospel traditions whereby remarriage becomes equated with adultery. For instance:

Whoever divorces his wife and marries another commits adultery against her; and if she divorces her husband and marries another, she commits adultery. (Mk 10.11–12)

But I say to you that anyone who divorces his wife, except on the ground of *porneia*, causes her to commit adultery; and whoever marries a divorced woman commits adultery. (Mt. 5.32)

Anyone who divorces his wife and marries another commits adultery, and whoever marries a woman divorced from her husband commits adultery. (Lk. 18.18)

Of course in the case of Matthew it seems that deemed sexual immorality is the exception: '. . . anyone who divorces his wife, except on the ground of *porneia* . . .' (Mt. 5.32). While there is an argument (accepted by this author) that Mark assumes the exception clause we find in Matthew (and remember Matthew adds the exception clause only to say that even this is too difficult), a widely held view is that Mark reflects an absolute prohibition of divorce. It is often suggested that such an absolute prohibition of divorce is found in the Dead Sea Scrolls:

> There are Belial's three nets about which Levi, son of Jacob spoke, by which he catches Israel and makes them appear before them like three types of justice. The first is fornication; the second, wealth; the third, defilement of the Temple. He who eludes one is caught in another and he who is freed from that, is caught in another. The builders of the wall who go after Zaw-Zaw is the preacher of whom he said: 'Assuredly they will preach' (Mic. 2.6) – are caught twice in fornication: by taking two wives in their lives, even though the principle of creation is 'male and female he made them' (Gen. 1.27), and the ones who went into the ark 'went in two by two in to the ark' (Gen. 7.9). And about the prince it is written: 'He should not multiply wives to himself' (Deut. 17.17). However, David had not read the sealed book of the law which was in the ark, for it had not been opened in Israel since the day of the death of Eleazar and of Jehoshua, and Joshua and the elders who worshipped Ashtaroth . . . (CD 4.15–5.4)

> On the day when they proclaim [him] king . . . And he shall take no other wife in addition to her for she alone will be with him all the days of her life. And if she dies, he shall take for himself another from his father's house, from his family. (11QT 57.2, 17–19)

The phrase, 'taking two wives in their lives' (CD 4.15–5.4), has been much contested. Does it mean divorce is absolutely prohibited? Or is it an emphatic defence of monogamy over against polygamy? Or perhaps even a critique of remarrying? Then there is the role of the ruler. In CD, the prince is not to have multiple wives, while in 11QT it seems as if the ruler cannot practise polygamy and should not divorce the woman during her life. Whatever we make of these texts we should add that the same documents from the Dead Sea Scrolls appear to assume the possibility of divorce, or the validity of divorcees, at least in certain circumstances:[4]

> And every vow of a widow or a divorcee, everything by which she binds herself formally will stand upon her, as everything which issues from her mouth . . . (11QT 54.4–5)

> If a man seduces a young virgin who is not betrothed, and she is permitted to him by the law and he lies with her and is discovered, then the man who lay with her shall give the girl's father fifty silver shekels and she will be (his) wife, since he raped her; and he cannot dismiss her all his days . . . (11QT 66.8–11)

> And no-one should make a deed of purchase or of sale without informing the Inspector of the camp; he shall proceed in consultation lest they e[rr. And likewise] with regard to [any]one who ma[rr]ies a wom[an] and [. . . in] consultation. And likewise, with regard to anyone who divorces . . . (CD 13.15–17)

It might have been observed that the there has been a significant gender imbalance in the presentation of the divorce texts. Clearly, the material presented concerns men divorcing women. However, both Mark (see above) and Paul mention the idea of women divorcing men. Paul, for instance, said, 'To the married I give this command – not I but the Lord – that the wife should not separate from her husband' (1 Cor. 7.10). It is often suggested that this reflects Roman rather than Jewish law because, so the argument goes, Jewish law did not allow the possibility of divorce. This is certainly the only concern written in Deut. 24.1–4 ('Suppose a man enters into marriage with a woman, but she does not please him . . . he writes her a certificate of divorce . . . '). This commonly held view, however, needs to be qualified, at least in terms of Judaism outside the Bible, because there are examples of women – particularly elite women – divorcing their husbands. In the fifth century BCE, the Jewish colony at Elephantine (an island on the Nile) allows the possibility of women divorcing husbands.[5] Closer to the time of the New Testament, Josephus gives a seemingly controversial example:

> Sometime afterwards Salome had occasion to quarrel with Costobarus and soon sent him a document dissolving their marriage which was not in accordance with Jewish law. For it is (only) the man who is permitted by us to do this, and not even a divorced woman may marry again on her own initiative unless her husband consents. Salome, however, did not chose to follow her country's law but acted on her own authority and repudiated her marriage . . .'
> (*Ant.* 15.259–260)

Papyrus Se'elim 13, a text from the Judean desert dating to the early second century CE, is another probable example of a woman divorcing her husband. According to the following reconstruction and translation by David Instone-Brewer we have a scribe writing on behalf of the wife:[6]

> I, Shelamzion, daughter of Joseph Qebshan, of Ein Gedi, with you, Eleazar son of Hananiah who had been her husband before this time, this is from her to you a bill of divorce and release. (lines 4–7)

There are more indirect examples in rabbinic literature relating to women leaving their husbands, or rather being able to petition for a divorce. These typically involve sex or at least that which is related by implication, namely, the not-particularly-pleasing husband. In some ways what we find is the gender reversal of Aqiba's finding-one-fairer argument. So women can petition for divorce if a husband has a particularly unpleasant job and different types of physical issues which are problematic for the wife:

> A man who suffers blemishes – they do not force him to put her away. Said Rabban Simeon b. Gamaliel, 'Under what circumstances? In the case of small blemishes. But in the case of major blemishes, they do force him to put her away'. And these are the ones whom they force to put her away: he who is afflicted with boils, or who has polypus, or who collects [dog excrement], or a coppersmith, or a tanner – whether these [blemishes] were present before they were married or whether after they were married they made their appearance. (*m. Ketub.* 7.2, 9–10)

Perhaps, and only perhaps, there is also an implication that the Samaritan woman in John 4 had some agency in previously getting divorced. At the very least she was active in going out and finding a man:

> Jesus said to her, 'Go, call your husband, and come back'. The woman answered him, 'I have no husband'. Jesus said to her, 'You are right in saying, "I have no husband"; for you have had five husbands, and the one you have now is not your husband. What you have said is true!' (Jn 4.16–18)

'EYE FOR AN EYE'

The famous 'eye for an eye' saying is an ancient principle but which for our purposes is grounded in Exod. 21.22–27:

> When people who are fighting injure a pregnant woman so that there is a miscarriage, and yet no further harm follows, the one responsible shall be fined what the woman's husband demands, paying as much as the judges determine. If any harm follows, then you shall give life for life, eye for eye, tooth for tooth, hand for

hand, foot for foot, burn for burn, wound for wound, stripe for stripe. When a slaveowner strikes the eye of a male or female slave, destroying it, the owner shall let the slave go, a free person, to compensate for the eye. If the owner knocks out a tooth of a male or female slave, the slave shall be let go, a free person, to compensate for the tooth.

This concept may well have been used to place a limit on vendettas but just how literally this verse and sentiment was and is to be interpreted was and is debated. The text itself is sufficiently ambiguous to generate the different interpretations. On the one hand, the context of Exod. 21.24 seems to point in a different direction. For example, in 21.22 we read, 'When, in the course of a brawl, a man knocks against a pregnant woman so that she has a miscarriage but suffers no further hurt, then the offender must pay whatever fine the woman's husband demands after assessment'. In the verses that follow, vv. 26–27, we then read, 'When a man strikes his slave or slave girl in the eye and destroys it, he shall let the slave girl go free in compensation for the eye. When he knocks out the tooth of a slave or a slave girl, he shall let the slave go free in compensation for the tooth'. The context emphatically reads the eye for an eye principle in terms of compensation.

On the other hand, at least read aside from its literary context, the language of eye for eye, foot for foot, burn for burn, wound for wound and so on does by itself seems black and white. Indeed, other Old Testament/Hebrew Bible texts appear to use the eye for an eye principle literally. One eye-watering example is from Deut. 25.11–12: 'When two men are fighting and the wife of one of them comes near to drag her husband clear of his opponent, if she puts out her hand and catches hold of the man's genitals, you shall cut off her hand and show her no mercy'. In the context of the Flood and some commandments with some authority in later Judaism, God said to Noah, 'He that sheds the blood of a man, for that man his blood shall be shed . . .' (Genesis 9.6).

So, it seems as if we have two views of how to interpret an 'eye for an eye': one is literal and physically violent; the other is not literal and financial/compensatory. With these different interpretations in the Bible itself, it is little wonder that different versions were championed. Some, such as Josephus, show the possibility of hedging bets and going for both interpretations:

He that maims anyone, let him undergo the like himself, and be deprived of the same member of which he has deprived the other, unless he that is maimed will accept money instead of it; for the law makes the sufferer the judge of the value of what he has suffered, and permits him to estimate it, unless he will be more severe. (*Ant.* 4.280)

However, in certain circles there was a hardening of the two interpretative categories in the sense that they were not necessarily as compatible as Josephus would have them. Rabbinic literature emphatically falls on the side of the non-violent and financial and compensatory. Translations of, and commentaries on, Exod. 21.24 make this quite clear. However, it does seem that the metaphorical reading was increasingly becoming the more dominant. In the Aramaic paraphrases of the Hebrew Bible/Old Testament (Targum), the idea of financial compensation is made explicit in the fairly loose translation. In Targum *Pseudo–Jonathan* to Exod. 21.24, for instance, we read, 'The value of an eye for an eye, the value of a tooth for a tooth, the value of a hand for a hand, the value of a foot for a foot . . .' In a rabbinic commentary this interpretation is spelled out if anything even clearer:

Eye for Eye. This means, monetary compensation for an eye. You interpret it to mean money for an eye . . . for any injuries resulting in a permanent defect and affecting chief organs and visible, though inflicted intentionally, one is subject only to payment of indemnity. (Mekilta de-Rabbi Ishmael on Exod. 21.24 [III.67–69])

In earlier rabbinic texts, the principle of compensation rather than violent retribution is clear, even if the text of Exod. 21.24 it is not:

> If a man wounded his fellow he thereby becomes liable on five accounts: for injury, for pain, for healing, for loss of time, and for indignity inflicted. 'For injury' – thus if he blinded his fellow's eye, cut off his hand, or broke his foot, [his fellow] is looked upon as if he were a slave to be sold in the market: they assess how much he was worth and how much he is worth now. 'For pain' – thus, if he burnt his fellow with a spit or a nail, even though it was on his finger-nail where it would leave no wound, they estimate how much money such a man would be willing to take to suffer so . . . (*m. Baba Qamma* 8.1)

It may be that the text of Exod. 21.24 is simply assumed to be underlying the discussion in this rabbinic passage. This Mishnah passage was interpreted and expanded in the Babylonian Talmud, *Baba Qamma* 83b–84a, where the reference to Exod. 21.24 is made quite explicit. Here there is a lengthy discussion of the validity of the financial compensation in relation to Exod. 21.24 and this interpretation is again emphatically favoured over the more literal interpretation. Numerous early rabbis are cited in favour of this interpretation with only one exception to which we will return. But anyway it begins like this:

> Why [pay compensation]? Does the Divine Law not say, 'Eye for an eye'? [Exodus 21.24] Why not take this literally to mean [putting out] the eye [of the offender]? – Let this not enter your mind . . . We speak of the effect of smiting implied in this text and the effect of smiting implied in the other text: just as smiting mentioned in the case of the beast refers to the payment of compensation, so also does smiting in the case of a man refer to the payment of compensation.

It would seem that Jesus stands in this tradition, at least as he is presented in the Gospels as opposing violent retribution in direct discussion of the 'eye for an eye' principle: 'Do not resist an evildoer. But if anyone strikes you on the right cheek, turn the other also' (Mt. 5.39; cf. Lk. 6.29).

Although the financial and compensatory view is the most common according to the texts we have, there was another minority view (again, at least according to the texts we have). *Jubilees*. 4.31, for instance, comments as follows on the death of Cain and also has the idea of using the same weapon which did the initial damage in revenge:

> . . . his house fell on him, and he died inside it and was killed by the stones of it; for with a stone he had killed Abel, and by a just retribution he was killed by a stone himself. There is a rule about this on the heavenly tablets, With the instrument with which one kills another man, with the same instrument shall he be killed: if he has done a particular injury to another man, the same injury shall be done to him.

There are hints that Sadducees held such a literal reading (*m. Mak.* 1.6) and the literal reading also found its way into the early rabbinic movement, although it was emphatically deemed a minority view. If we return to the later Babylonian Talmud text, *Baba Qamma* 83b–84a, and the lengthy discussion of the validity of the financial compensation in relation to Exod. 21.24, we find the one dissenting voice in R. Eliezer (late first century CE) who was said to have favoured the literal interpretation:

> It was taught: R. Eliezer said: Eye for an eye literally refers to the eye [of the offender]. Literally, you say? Could R. Eliezer be against all those early rabbis [listed above]? (b. *Baba Qamma* 83b–84a)

While it is certainly fair to stress the stark differences between the two interpretations, we should add that the differences start to break down when we think of punishment in the afterlife of those deemed wrongdoers. This was a common enough view in early Judaism and, of course, the New Testament itself, including the Gospel of Matthew who not only includes Jesus' rejection of a violent interpretation of the 'eye for an eye' principle but also sentiments such as the following:

> Not everyone who says to me, 'Lord, Lord', will enter the kingdom of heaven, but only the one who does the will of my Father in heaven. On that day many will say to me, 'Lord, Lord, did we not prophesy in your name, and cast out demons in your name, and do many deeds of power in your name?' Then I will declare to them, 'I never knew you; go away from me, you evildoers'. (Mt. 7.21–23; cf. Mt. 6.14–15)

The rejection of the violent interpretation of the 'eye for an eye' principle clearly applied to this life in the here and now, just as the rejection of death for Sabbath breakers and adulterers was. Presumably one eye was on societal cohesion and the prevention of killing far too many people in society in the rejection of the violent interpretation. It may be significant that the violent interpretation is associated with the sectarian views of the book of *Jubilees*, a text associated with the Dead Sea Scrolls.

OATHS AND VOWS

Following E. P. Sanders, we could use the following definition of the distinction between oaths and vows: 'Oaths were important for society because they guaranteed a word or action by appealing to God and calling down his curse if it was broken . . . A vow is essentially a promise, with a guarantee of divine sanction if it is not fulfilled'.[7] However, in this section oaths and vows will be lumped together, not least because they are so obviously similar categories. Oaths and vows are also something of a legal grey area. They are certainly present in biblical Law:

> Or when any of you utter aloud a rash oath for a bad or a good purpose, whatever people utter in an oath, and are unaware of it, when you come to know it, you shall in any of these be guilty. When you realize your guilt in any of these, you shall confess the sin that you have committed. And you shall bring to the Lord, as your penalty for the sin that you have committed, a female from the flock, a sheep or a goat, as a sin-offering; and the priest shall make atonement on your behalf for your sin. (Lev. 5.4–6)

> If you make a vow to the Lord your God, do not postpone fulfilling it; for the Lord your God will surely require it of you, and you would incur guilt. (Deut. 23.21; cf. Num. 30)

However, unlike commandments to observe the Sabbath, these are not commandments to undertake oaths any more than Deuteronomy 24 commands divorce. In other words, there is no commandment along the lines of 'you shall (or shall not) make an oath or vow' any more than there is a commandment 'you shall divorce'. Instead what we are dealing with is how oaths and vows can be dealt with in practice. Avoidance of oaths and vows was not against scripture; on the contrary avoidance was potentially a very good thing. For once made, if the Law said they should be fulfilled then they should be fulfilled. The Deuteronomy 23 passage cited above continues:

> If you make a vow to the Lord your God, do not postpone fulfilling it; for the Lord your God will surely require it of you, and you would incur guilt. But if you refrain from vowing, you will not incur guilt. Whatever your lips utter you must diligently perform, just as you have freely vowed to the Lord with your own mouth. (Deut. 23.21–23)

The safest option, so to speak, of avoidance of oaths and vows was certainly present by the time of the New Testament. As Philo put it, 'Next to not swearing at all, the second best thing is to keep one's oath; for by the mere fact of swearing at all, the swearer shows that there is some suspicion of his not being trustworthy'. (*Decal.* 84). These sorts of sentiments were especially associated with the Essenes, at least in the eyes of Josephus and Philo:

> . . . whatever they [the Essenes] say also is firmer than an oath; but swearing is avoided by them, and they esteem it worse than perjury; for they say that he who cannot be believed without [swearing by] God is already condemned. (*War* 2.135)

> Their love of God they show by a multitude of proofs, by religious purity constant and unbroken throughout their lives, by abstinence from oaths, by veracity, by their belief that the Godhead is the cause of all good things and nothing bad . . . (*Every Good Man is Free* 84)

Here we have something similar to Jesus' words according to Matthew: 'do not swear at all' (Mt. 5.34). However, Jesus' words do seem to qualify this when he says, 'Let your word be "Yes, Yes" or "No, No"; anything more than this comes from the evil one' and this may bring him in line with those said to be critical of people who made elaborate oaths and vows (Mt. 5.37).[8] Similarly, if we follow the view that the Essenes were the group behind the Dead Sea Scrolls, then the descriptions given by Philo and Josephus of the Essenes' view on swearing oaths are also to be qualified by the Scrolls themselves.

> Concerning an oath. What he said: 'You shall not do justice with your (own) hand' (1 Sam. 25.26): whoever forces the making of an oath in the open field, not in the presence of judges or at their command, has done justice for himself with his hand. Every lost

object about which it is was stolen – its owner should make a maledictory oath; whoever hears it, if he knows and does not say it, is guilty . . . (CD 9.9–12)

Whoever enters the council of the Community enters the covenant of God in the presence of all who freely volunteer. He shall swear a binding oath to revert to the Law of Moses, according to all that he commanded . . . (1QS 5.8)

If the logic of the laws and sentiments concerning the swearing of oaths and vows is taken to its logical conclusion – the less-than-safe option, so to speak – then this puts the swearer in a potentially difficult situation. One of the most gruesome examples of this is the story of Jephthah's daughter in Judges 11.30–40. Jephthah swears the following: 'If you will give the Ammonites into my hand, then whoever comes out of the doors of my house to meet me when I return victorious from the Ammonites, shall be the Lord's, to be offered up by me as a burnt offering' (Judges 11.30). Jephthah got what he desired only for his daughter to be the first person to walk through his door and so the poor girl has to be sacrificed. Little wonder some people thought it best to avoid swearing oaths and vows altogether. As Jesus put the magnitude of the matter, 'whoever swears by the altar, swears by it and by everything on it; and whoever swears by the sanctuary, swears by it and by the one who dwells in it; and whoever swears by heaven, swears by the throne of God and by the one who is seated upon it' (Mt. 23.20–22). Indeed, the logic of avoiding oaths and vows because they are in the name of God in order to prevent God's name being profaned may well be the same logic Mt. 5.33–35 as a whole:

Again, you have heard that it was said to those of ancient times, 'You shall not swear falsely, but carry out the vows you have made to the Lord'. But I say to you, Do not swear at all, either by heaven, for it is the throne of God, or by the earth, for it is his footstool, or by Jerusalem, for it is the city of the great King.

Avoid swearing and you avoid swearing falsely. Problem solved.

One such disaster in the New Testament is in the story of the death of John the Baptist (Mk 6.17–29). Once Herod Antipas has been wooed by the dancing daughter, she gets an offer from Herod Antipas she can hardly refuse: "'Ask me for whatever you wish, and I will give it." And he solemnly swore to her, "Whatever you ask me, I will give you, even half of my kingdom"' (Mk 6.22–23). By swearing to carry out his promise Antipas was bound and predictably the dancing daughter asks for the head of John the Baptist, a man who was starting to impress Herod Antipas. Many scholars have noted that the story of the death of John the Baptist has striking similarities with the story of Esther (cf. Est. 5.3; 7.2) and so we might note that the king in the Greek 'A' version of the book of Est. 8.7 (based on the Hebrew Est. 7.5) 'swore that she [Esther] should tell him who had behaved so arrogantly as to do this, and with an oath he undertook to do for her whatever she wished'. Notice how in the Markan story Herod Antipas could not get out of the situation once he had sworn: 'The king was deeply grieved; yet out of regard for his oaths and for the guests, he did not want to refuse her' (6.26). The reference to the guests combined with the oath may point to a broader social acceptance – as well as direct witnesses – of the significance of swearing oaths. Indeed, according to Josephus, the Roman Emperor Gaius Caligula had to carry out that which he swore in front of distinguished guests. The context in Josephus is of the then political leader of the Jews, Agrippa, audaciously asking Gaius Caligula not to put a statue of himself in the Jerusalem Temple. Not unlike the dancing daughter, Agrippa was smart enough to play on the importance of oaths in a situation which could have cost him his life:

And thus did Agrippa venture to cast the die upon this occasion, so great was the affair in his opinion, and in reality, though he knew how dangerous a thing it was so to speak; for, had not Gaius approved of it, it had tended to no less than the loss of his life. So Gaius, who was mightily taken with Agrippa's obliging behaviour, and, on other accounts, thinking it a dishonourable thing to be guilty of falsehood before so many witnesses . . . (*Ant.* 18.298–299)

Issues relating to oaths and vows were, as ever, open to interpretation and dispute. The tension between scripture and tradition is mentioned in Mk 7.9–13 where Jesus is said to have criticized Pharisees and scribes for rejecting 'the commandment of God' in favour of their 'tradition'. The commandment of God is honouring parents (Exod. 20.12/Deut. 5.16) and the tradition deemed to be contrasting is described as follows: 'But you say that if anyone tells father or mother, "Whatever support you might have had from me is Qorban" (that is, an offering to God) – then you no longer permit doing anything for a father or mother . . .' (Mk 7.11–12). Precisely what *qorban* would have meant at the time of Jesus is not entirely clear but, thanks to Mark, we can at least say it was something like a gift and from later rabbinic literature suggest that it was dedicated in someway to God and/or the Temple through a vow or oath.

It seems as if the Jesus of Mark's Gospel would, in the general sense, have been supported by a broad spectrum of rabbinic opinion:

[If] he saw people eating figs [belonging to him] and said, 'Lo, they are *qorban* to you!' And they turned out to be his father and brothers, and there were others with them – the House of Shammai say, 'They are permitted, and those with them are prohibited'. And the House of Hillel say, 'These and those [men] are permitted [to eat the figs]'. (m. *Nedarim* 3.2)

However, and even if not quite as extreme as the opponents constructed in the polemic of the Markan Jesus, in certain cases dedications which involved parents were not to be overturned. Compare the following:

There was someone from Beth Horon whose father was prohibited by vow from deriving benefit from him. And he [the man from Beth Horon] was marrying off his son, and he said to his fellow,

'The courtyard and the banquet are given over to you as a gift. But they are before you only so that father may come and eat with us at the banquet'. The other party said, 'Now if they really are mine, then lo, they are consecrated to heaven!' He said to him, 'You did not give me what's yours except so that you and your father could eat and drink and make friends again, and so the sin [for violating the oath] could rest on his head!' Now the case came before the sages. They ruled, 'any act of donation which is not so [given] that, if one sanctified it to Heaven, it is sanctified, is no act of donation'. (m. *Nedarim* 5.6)

Of course, this example involves the idea of a conditional gift and ought not to be pushed in the direction of a strict interpretation in the sense of the Markan Jesus' polemics against Pharisees in Mk 7.9–13. Philo also gives us the reverse situation whereby a father can refrain from giving to his son, in addition to his wife and in addition to a ruler giving to subjects:

Each individual is master of his possessions unless he has solemnly named the name of God over them declaring that he has given them to God. And if he has merely made a chance verbal promise of them he must not touch or handle them, but hold himself at once debarred from them all . . . even with his own, I repeat, a chance word of dedication spoken unawares deprives him of them all and if he repents or denies his promise his life is forfeit also. The same holds of any other persons over whom he has authority. If a man has devoted his wife's sustenance to a sacred purpose he must refrain from giving her that sustenance; so with a father's gifts to his son or a ruler's to his subjects. The chief and most perfect way of releasing dedicated property is by the priest refusing it, for he is empowered by God to accept it or not . . . (*Hypoth.* 7.3–5)

Notice also that Philo adds that such practices in language which can be classified as expansion and interpretation of the Law and which Mark described as 'tradition' in contrast to the biblical Law in

Mk 7.9–13: 'Besides these there is a host of other things which belong to unwritten customs and institutions or are contained in the laws themselves' (*Hypoth.* 7.6).

SUMMARY

Ideally, divorce was deemed to be a necessary evil and marriage was deemed to be a good thing. However, divorce was permitted in certain circumstances thanks to the exception that if a husband finds 'something objectionable' about his wife he can divorce her. By now it should be no surprise that 'something objectionable' needed further definition. The definitions differed, from the 'strict' view that divorce is permissible in the case of something like adultery to the less strict views such as a wife burning the food. It seems as if the New Testament texts are more in line with the 'strict' views. The New Testament texts also seem as if they are in line with a view which attacked divorce for the sake of remarriage. While there is a notable emphasis on the agency of the husband in discussions of divorce laws, the wife is not entirely neglected. There are some texts which suggest wives were divorcing their husbands and certain rabbinic texts suggest that a husband could be forced to divorce his wife.

In the case of an 'eye for an eye', biblical Law is ambiguous: it is possible to interpret this principle as a literal case of violent retribution and a less literal case of financial (or equivalent) compensation. However, from the evidence we have it seems as if the dominant view, followed by New Testament texts, was that 'eye for an eye' ought to be read in terms of compensation and definitely not violent retribution. In the case of oaths and vows, there is no biblical law which commands oaths and vows but there are discussions of what needs to be done in carrying out oaths and vows. In fact, biblical Law gives the chance to avoid oaths and vows and avoid breaking them and some people were believed to have avoided them altogether, not least because keeping them could lead to all sorts of problems. As ever, there are debates over details but it seems that the New Testament texts do nothing unknown in early Judaism.

CHAPTER 5

CIRCUMCISION, FAMILY AND INTERACTION WITH GENTILES

While in sociological terms, 'ethnicity' might refer to a specific social group which might be deemed to have 'obvious' ethnic characteristics, with links to specific place of origin, biological connections, specific customs and so on, these can break down on closer inspection. Outsider perceptions do not necessarily correspond to insider perceptions (do some of the famous stereotypes about Arabs or Scots really correspond to some 'truth' or to Arab or Scottish self-identities?) and insider perceptions may differ from one another. In some ways, this questioning of hard and fast views corresponds with the diversity of opinion this book has pointed out in relation to Jewish legal debates. This chapter will now look at some of the issues relating to Jewish ethnicity, largely from insider perspectives, in particular some of the more prominent discussions from the ancient sources such as biological links and family, circumcision and becoming a Jew, social interaction between Jews and Gentiles and Jewish perceptions of Gentiles. I stress that this chapter will only cover *some* of the issues relating to ethnicity. I will not cover, for instance, the lively debate over whether geographical terms, such as 'Israelite' and 'Judean', are historically more suitable than 'Jew' because, for obvious reasons, I want to keep the focus of this book and this chapter on legal and quasi-legal debates and related issues in the New Testament.[1]

IMPORTANCE OF FAMILY

Family was and is intricately linked in with issues of ethnicity and what is deemed to make a Jew a Jew. Today we might often think of the widespread idea of someone's Jewish identity being dependent on having a Jewish mother, a view developed in rabbinic literature but which appears to have been unknown earlier in the times when the New Testament documents were being written.[2] But whatever views were present in the first century, the general issue of parental links was, obviously, deemed to be of some importance in defining someone as a Jew.

Indeed, it is one logical conclusion that if ethnicity was going to be so important, then family and blood lineage would play an important role in early Jewish thought. The Ten Commandments are fairly blunt about this: 'Honour your father and your mother, so that your days may be long in the land that the LORD your God is giving you' (Exod. 20.12; cf. Deut. 5.16). According to Mark, Jesus emphatically endorsed this biblical commandment in contrast to the 'traditions' of his opponents: 'For Moses said, "Honour your father and your mother"; and, "Whoever speaks evil of father or mother must surely die"' (Mk 7.10). In fact devotion to parents could be seen as one of the most important commandments of them all. According to Josephus,

> The law ordains also, that parents should be honoured immediately after God himself, and delivers that son who does not requite them for the benefits he has received from them, but is deficient on any such occasion, to be stoned. It also says, that the young men should pay due respect to every elder, since God is the oldest of all beings. (*Apion* 2.206)

Among the kinds of duties expected in honouring parents is as basic as the burial of the dead parents. Unsurprisingly, then, we get the following concerns brought up as in the following example from Tobit 6.15: 'So now, since I am the only son my father has, I am afraid that I may die and bring my father's and mother's life down to their grave, grieving for me – and they have no other son to bury them'. Similar sentiments are found on the lips of one would-be disciple, who said, according to Matthew and Luke, 'Lord, first let me go and bury my father' (Mt. 8.21; Lk. 9.59).

There were exceptions in biblical Law to the burial of the father. The High Priest is not allowed to come into contact with a dead body, not even his father or mother (Lev. 21.11), while elsewhere in biblical Law a special vow could be undertaken, the Nazirite vow, which, among other things, entailed the avoidance of contact with a corpse, including the corpse of a given close relative such as father, mother, brother, and sister (Num. 6.6). Though it is common in scholarship to believe these exceptions to have been weakened by the time of Jesus, at least in relation to the burial of parents, in fact these exceptions were, by Philo at least, reinforced with further explanation.[3] Of the High Priest, Philo claimed:

. . . but the high priest he [Moses] absolutely forbade to mourn in any case whatever; and may we not say that this was rightly done? For as to the ministrations which belong to the other priests, one individual can perform them instead of another, so that, even if some be in mourning, still none of the usual observances need be omitted; but there is no one besides the high priest himself, who is permitted to perform his duties instead of him . . . and God commands the high priest neither to rend his clothes over his very nearest relations when they die, nor to take from his head the ensign of the priesthood, nor in short to depart from the holy place on any plea of mourning, that, showing proper respect to the place, and to the sacred ornaments with which he himself is crowned, he may show himself superior to pity, and pass the whole of his life exempt from all sorrow. (*Spec. Leg.* 1.113–115)

Of the Nazirite vow, Philo claimed:

. . . they are commanded to keep their body pure and undefiled, so as not even to approach their parents if they are dead, nor their brothers; piety overcoming the natural good will and affection towards their relations and dearest friends, and it is both honourable and expedient that piety should at all times prevail. (*Spec. Leg.* 1.250)

Significantly, when rabbis discussed the exceptions for the High Priest and the Nazirite vow, they did not include parents:

A high priest and a Nazir do not contract corpse uncleanness on account of [burying even] their close relatives. But they do contract corpse uncleanness on account of a neglected corpse. [If] they were going along the way and found a neglected corpse – R. Eliezer says, 'Let a high priest contract corpse uncleanness, but let a Nazir not contract corpse uncleanness'. And the Sages say, 'Let a Nazir contract corpse uncleanness, but let a high priest not contract corpse uncleanness'. (*m. Nazir* 7.1)

We are back in the realm of the debates over what to do with an abandoned corpse and the avoidance impurity as seen previously in the case of the parable of the Good Samaritan (see Chapter 3).

But on the exalting of family, there were qualifications made.[4] According to Josephus, Moses stressed that family must come a very firm second behind the commandments: 'And let them be to you venerable, and contended for more earnestly by you than your own children and your own wives' (*Ant.* 3.86–88). Still, versions of this sort of view could remain controversial for some if it affected procreation, certainly according to at least one later rabbinic source. Simeon b. Azzai got some abuse for downplaying family to the extent of not getting married: 'The Sages: "You [Simeon ben Azzai] preach well, but do not practise your preaching." Said Simeon b. Azzai: "My soul is in love with the Torah. The world can be kept going by others"' (*b. Yeb.* 63b). One logical outworking of a downplaying of family for the study of the commandments would lead to a sort of 'fictive kinship' when carried out with others, as in the case of the Essenes who seem to have come to a collective version of Simeon b. Azzai's argument. The following ancient exercise in male bonding and paranoia about women could lend itself to all sorts of interesting analyses:

> Essenes . . . are Jews by birth, and seem to have a greater affection for one another than the other sects have . . . They neglect wedlock, but select other persons' children, while they are pliable, and fit for learning, and esteem them to be of their kindred, and form them according to their own manners. They do not absolutely deny the fitness of marriage, and the succession of mankind thereby continued; but they guard against the lascivious behaviour of women, and are persuaded that none of them preserve their fidelity to one man . . . everyone's possessions are intermingled with everyone's possessions; and so there is, as it were, one patrimony among all the brethren. (*War* 2.119–122; see also *Ant.* 18.18–22)

This tradition of 'fictive kinship' was no doubt of some importance for Paul when he had to deal bring together Jews and Gentiles and where Jewish ethnicity may well have been fine for those born Jewish (Rom. 9–11) but not for those who were not. 'Fictive kinship' was one way of emphasizing a united Christian movement (think of the regular use of 'brothers').

Jesus' apparently 'radical' sayings on family as recorded in the Gospels may well stand more in the tradition of 'fictive kinship' while also maintaining the importance of biological family links. For instance, when Jesus' mother and brothers wish to see him, he responds, 'Who are my mother and my brothers?' and then looks at those sat around him, adding, 'Here are my mother and my brothers! Whoever does the will of God is my brother and sister and mother' (Mk 3.33–35). This is close in sentiment to the Essenes and perhaps Simeon b. Azzai. Like both of those it seems as if Jesus still managed to see family as a good thing; we should also not forget that Jesus in the same Gospel emphatically criticized opponents for not caring for parents and overriding the commandment to honour parents (Mk 7.10).

Mark also looks forward to a time when those who have left 'house or brothers or sisters or mother or father or children or fields' will receive 'hundredfold now in this age – houses, brothers and sisters, mothers and children, and fields with persecutions – and in the age to come eternal life' (Mk 10.29–30).

Elsewhere, in Matthew's Gospel, it seems as if the prioritizing of family is brought to the fore, as in the following where the comparison presumably only works if family is regarded highly: 'Whoever loves father or mother more than me is not worthy of me; and whoever loves son or daughter more than me is not worthy of me' (Mt. 10.37). Luke's parallel version of this saying appears harsher: 'Whoever comes to me and does not hate father and mother, wife and children, brothers and sisters, yes, and even life itself, cannot be my disciple' (Lk. 14.26). It is likely, however, that Luke is not too far removed from Matthew here because the Greek verb 'hate' is not necessarily as strong as the English and is used to translate the Hebrew (and Aramaic) equivalent where the sense is 'love-less' (cf. Gen. 29.31–35; Deut. 21.15–17). It is possible that, as some have suggested, Matthew and Luke have independently translated the weaker Aramaic equivalent in their own different but equally valid ways.[5]

And then there is Jesus' response to the would-be disciple who wants to bury his father, 'Let the dead bury their dead' (Mt. 8.22/ Lk. 9.60). We should note from the start that the implication of this saying is that the dead father would not be left unburied: others would bury him. Again, this saying may well be in the realm of prioritizing the role of family for what are deemed more pressing issues in the here and now, or possibly something similar to the exception for the Nazirite vow or (less likely) High Priest.[6] To use a slightly anachronistic comparison, and reapplying the situation to one more overtly concerning 'justice', Terry Eagleton, responding to Richard Dawkins, implies that such views on family should not suggest kidnapping by religious cults because such views do not see 'that movements for justice cut across traditional blood ties, as well as across ethnic, social, and national divisions. Justice is thicker than blood'.[7]

As Jesus was growing up, the urban centres of Sepphoris and Tiberias were being rebuilt and built. As the typical economic pattern in the ancient world was one of urban centres extracting the resources from the surrounding villages (such as Nazareth), these building projects would almost inevitably have led to changes in lifestyle. Issues of relating to dislocation are mentioned by Josephus (*Ant.* 18.36–38) and it may well be of some significance that there was a full scale revolt against Rome (66–70 CE) where hatred was levelled at Sepphoris and Tiberias (*Life* 30, 39, 66–8, 99, 374–84). At the very least we can say that change was not welcomed by all and, as Halvor Moxnes has shown, such economic changes would probably have meant that changes for conventional households would have led to many young men not heading households as would traditionally have been expected of them.[8] As we have seen, the Gospels indicate that there was some kind of fragmentation of household (e.g. Mk 3.20–22, 31–35; 10.29–30; Mt. 8.22/Lk. 9.60; Mt. 10.34–36/Lk. 12.51–53/ Thom. 16.1–4; Mt. 10.37/Lk. 14.26), and the social context of Galilee as Jesus was growing up, combined with traditions of putting family in its place, may help explain the relatively intense concern for alternative family in the Gospels.

CIRCUMCISION AND DIFFERENCE

For men, circumcision was crucial in defining who might be a Jew: 'You shall circumcise the flesh of your foreskins, and it shall be a sign of the covenant between me and you' (Gen. 17.11). On one level, circumcision was relatively simple, assuming the person in case was an eight-day-old baby boy (Gen. 17.12) where hopefully all would be well. This was not so easy for an adult male wishing to become a Jew. Circumcision would have been extremely painful to the extent of life-threatening so it is no surprise that we find people taking on Jewish ideas but with circumcision being a distinctive and perhaps ultimate step. This seems to be implied in the following example from Josephus: '. . . thus were all these men barbarously murdered, excepting Metilius; for when he entreated for mercy, and promised that he would turn Jew, and be circumcised, they saved him alive' (*War* 2.454). The verb used here is literally 'to Judaize' and notice how it is in distinction from circumcision which appears to be something else needed to go the full way to becoming a Jew according to this line of thought (LXX Esth. 8.17; *War.* 2.462–463). It might be significant that Paul uses the same verb 'to Judaize' when he criticizes Peter for withdrawing from eating with Gentile Christians after previously he would eat with them: 'But when I saw that they were not acting consistently with the truth of the gospel, I said to Cephas before them all, "If you, though a Jew, live like a Gentile and not like a Jew, how can you compel the Gentiles to live like Jews (literally: 'to Judaize')?"' (Gal. 2.14). Some scholars have argued that the use of 'to Judaize' is evidence that the dispute between Peter and Paul concerned Jewish practices surrounding food laws and not circumcision.[9] That food laws and not circumcision was the issue is supported in the light of Jewish sources which consistently describe food issues as a potential problem for Jewish-Gentile interaction, as we will see later in this chapter.

The issue of forced circumcision of households occasionally arises when a Jew, for instance, gains slaves thereby implying that, for some, conversion was required before technically becoming a Jew. There is a scriptural example referring to the specific context of Passover which could, and presumably was, read to apply to more general situations. According to Exod. 12.48, 'If an alien who resides with you wants to celebrate the Passover to the Lord, all his males shall be circumcised . . . he shall be regarded as a native of the land'. In the Palestinian Talmud we find the following theoretical example of circumcising Gentile slaves if they belong to a Jewish slave owner: 'R. Isaac bar Nahman in the name of R. Joshua b. Levi: A man once bought a city of uncircumcised slaves from a Gentile on condition that he would circumcise them, but they retracted' (*y. Yeb.* 8, 8d).

Another different type of theoretical example is found in a rabbinic retelling of the book of Jonah. The response of the Gentile sailors to

God's dramatic actions Jonah 1.15–16 has what might be a problem for an observant Jew: 'So they picked up Jonah, threw him into the sea, and the sea stopped its raging. Then the men feared the LORD greatly, and they offered a sacrifice to the LORD and made vows'. A sacrifice at sea might seem a little too pagan for some Jewish sensibilities such as those underlying the rabbinic *Pirqe de Rabbi Eliezer* and so 'sacrifices' gets reinterpreted to mean circumcision and thus everyone made vows to bring their children 'and all belonging to him' to the God of Jonah (*Pirqe de Rabbi Eliezer* 10).

While the above examples may have been theoretical it seems as if on the ground there was circumcision of households occurring, hence the following piece of Roman law which restricts circumcision to Jewish sons only and thus assuming cases where Gentiles were being circumcised by Jews:

MODESTINUS, *Rules, book* 6: By a rescript of the deified Pius [Roman emperor Antoninus Pius, ruled 138–161 CE] it is allowed only to Jews to circumcise their own sons; a person not of that religion who does so suffers the penalty of one carrying out a castration. (*Digesta* 48.8.11)

Issues of circumcision unsurprisingly turn up when Josephus discusses male converts to Judaism. The most prominent example is Josephus'[s] story of the conversion of Izates and the royal house of Adiabene (*Ant.* 20.34–48). Through the influence of a Jewish merchant called Ananias, women at court worshipped the Jewish god and they were in turn able to influence the male Izates. As Izates, who would become king, took on more aspects of Jewish practice this inevitably meant that the issue of circumcision would be raised. Izates was of the opinion that he could not be 'thoroughly a Jew unless he were circumcised, he was ready to have it done' (*Ant.* 20.38). Izates' mother, herself interested in Jewish practices, disagreed for political reasons arguing 'this thing would bring him into danger' as it would displease his subjects who 'would never bear to be ruled over by

THE NEW TESTAMENT AND JEWISH LAW

a Jew' (*Ant.* 20.39). Ananias agreed with Helena, not least because he might get some of the blame, conveniently adding the argument that Izates 'might worship God without being circumcised, even though he did resolve to follow the Jewish law entirely, which worship of God was of a superior nature to circumcision . . . God would forgive him, though he did not perform the operation, while it was omitted out of necessity, and for fear of his subjects' (*Ant.* 20.41). A not entirely convinced Izates initially accepted this ruling, before a strict Galilean Jew called Eleazar urged circumcision based on a kind of logic that it is too convenient to avoid the difficult bits, adding, 'How long will you continue uncircumcised? But if you have not yet read the law about circumcision, and do not know how great impiety you are guilty of by neglecting it, read it now' (*Ant.* 20.45). The surgeon was then summoned and the job was done. A later rabbinic recalling of the story of Izates conveys the problem well:

> Once Monabaz and Izates, the sons of King Ptolemy, were sitting and reading the book of Genesis. When they came to the verse, 'And you shall be circumcised' [Gen. 17.11] one turned his face towards the wall and commenced to weep, and the other turned his face to the wall and commenced to weep. Then each went and had himself circumcised. (*Gen. R.* 46.10)

Clearly, then, social pressures could influence decisions on circumcision. No such difficulties for women, of course, and it is probably significant in this respect that Josephus can speak of groups and large numbers of (elite) women interested in, or converted to, Judaism. We have just seen the example of women at the court of Izates. At the beginning of the Jewish uprising against Rome (66–70 CE), Josephus describes how husbands in Damascus wanted to destroy Jewish people yet 'their only fear was of their own wives who, with few exceptions, had all become converts to the Jewish religion, and so their efforts were mainly directed to keeping the secret from them' (*War* 2.560–561). Women discussed by Josephus tend to be elite women (e.g. *Ant.* 18.81–84) and this qualification provides further reasons for the possibility of conversion. Death of the husband would be one way but there are instances of elite women playing a more active intellectual role in the household. The first century CE Roman thinker Musonius Rufus argued that a woman trained in philosophy is a better manager of a household (Musonius Rufus, frag. 3). Without the problematic circumcision, Judaism was one such option for prominent women.

Similarly it might be the case that non-Jews who also practised circumcision were able to convert to Judaism with the ease of people who know they do not have to go through the operation as an adult. Jewish writers were certainly familiar with non-Jews being circumcised. For example, Philo wrote of the different people circumcised with a particularly interesting explanation:

> But that here it was thought fit that man should be circumcised out of a provident care for his mind without any previous infirmity is plain, since not the Jews alone, but also the Egyptians, and Arabians, and Ethiopians, and nearly all the nations who live in the southern parts of the world, down to the torrid zone are circumcised. (*Ques. Gen.* 3.48)

That the potential converts to Judaism from such places would not need circumcision according to some Jews close to the time of the New Testament is perhaps implied by the polemic of *Jubilees*:

> And now I shall announce to you that the sons of Israel will deny this ordinance [circumcision] and they will not circumcise their sons according to all of this law because some of the flesh of their circumcision they will leave in the circumcision of their sons. And all the sons of Beliar will leave their sons without circumcising just as they were born. (*Jub.* 15.33)

Clearly, then, circumcision must be done correctly and, from this perspective, it is unlikely that a non-Jewish circumcision would survive such rigorous scrutiny. Yet we also get stories such as that of the Arab Syllaeus who was due to marry into Jewish aristocracy but would not convert because he would be stoned to death by his own people (*Ant.* 16.225). As circumcision is not mentioned (and in contrast to the story of Izates), and as Syllaeus is described as an 'Arab', a perfectly reasonable piece of speculation might be that this is because Syllaeus would already have been circumcised.[10]

But in light of what we have seen concerning non-Arab, non-Egyptian and non-Ethiopian male converts to Judaism, it is perhaps little surprise that circumcision became a flash point for earliest Christianity when it started to attract Gentiles. In Galatians, Paul is in fierce debate with those who believe Gentile Christians should be circumcised to the extent he says, 'I wish those who unsettle you would castrate themselves!' (Gal. 5.12). In his later letter to the Romans, Paul's tone may be more conciliatory but still the issue of circumcision has to be discussed and Paul tries to work out a position whereby circumcision is not required and attempts to argue for a lack of logic in the position of stressing the importance of circumcision to become (effectively) a Christian in a more radical form of argument of those trying to dissuade Izates:

> Circumcision indeed is of value if you obey the law; but if you break the law, your circumcision has become uncircumcision. So, if those who are uncircumcised keep the requirements of the law, will not their uncircumcision be regarded as circumcision? Then those who are physically uncircumcised but keep the law will condemn you that have the written code and circumcision but break the law. For a person is not a Jew who is one outwardly, nor is true circumcision something external and physical. Rather, a person is a Jew who is one inwardly, and real circumcision is a matter of the heart – it is spiritual and not literal. (Rom. 2.25–29)

We might compare the debate in Acts 15 where 'certain individuals' from Judea and Pharisees believed that Gentiles converting to the new Christian movement needed to be circumcised, with the Pharisees adding that the Law of Moses needed to be observed (Acts 15.1, 5). In contrast, the decision taken at the meeting recorded in Acts 15 was that circumcision – and indeed much of the Law it would seem – was not required of Gentile converts. Here we might also compare the position of those dismissed by Philo who allegorize circumcision to the point of the physical being unnecessary, as discussed in Chapter 1. That Philo has to react also says something of the controversial nature of avoiding physical circumcision:

> For there are some men, who, looking upon written laws as symbols of things appreciable by the intellect . . . But now men living solitarily by themselves as if they were in a desert, or else as if they were mere souls unconnected with the body, and as if they had no knowledge of any city, or village, or house, or in short of any company of men whatever, overlook what appears to the many to be true, and seek for plain naked truth by itself, whom the sacred scripture teaches not to neglect a good reputation, and not to break through any established customs which divine men of greater wisdom than any in our time have enacted or established . . . nor because the rite of circumcision is an emblem of the excision of pleasures and of all the passions, and of the destruction of that impious opinion, according to which the mind has imagined itself to be by itself competent to produce offspring, does it follow that we are to annul the law which has been enacted about circumcision . . . (*Mig.* 89, 90, 92)

That people would feel so strongly about circumcision was not simply because it was mentioned so emphatically in Genesis. One of the most famous and retold aspects of Jewish history was the Maccabean crisis (see Chapter 1) where circumcision became outlawed and perceived as a distinctive marker of who was a Jew and where, in the build up to the crisis, the removal of the marks of circumcision could be perceived to be a supreme act of disloyalty to

Judaism. Look at the shock in sources where Jews remove the marks of circumcision and how it was seen by some as a key aspect of identifying a Jew:

> In those days certain renegades came out from Israel and misled many, saying, 'Let us go and make a covenant with the Gentiles around us, for since we separated from them many disasters have come upon us'. This proposal pleased them, and some of the people eagerly went to the king, who authorised them to observe the ordinances of the gentiles. So they built a gymnasium in Jerusalem, according to gentile custom, and removed the mark of circumcision, and they abandoned the holy covenant. They joined with the gentiles and sold themselves to do evil. (1 Macc. 1.11–15)

It is already clear that, for the writer of 1 Maccabees at least, the removal of circumcision is the removal of something which makes a person Jewish and an act which makes a person Gentile. This line of thought, if anything, is further emphasized in Josephus' retelling:

> Therefore they desired his permission to build them a gymnasium at Jerusalem. And when he had given them permission, they also hid the circumcision of their genitals, that even when they were naked they might appear to be Greeks. Accordingly, they abandoned all the customs that belonged to their own country, and imitated the practices of the other nations. (*Ant.* 12.241)

This view of defining Jew and Gentile through circumcision is an assumption which could be made in earliest Christianity, even when the Jew Paul was writing for a largely Gentile audience in Galatia. Paul recalls how he had been 'entrusted with the gospel for the uncircumcised, just as Peter had been entrusted with the gospel for the circumcised' and how the leaders in Jerusalem agreed that Barnabas and Paul should go to the Gentiles and they to the circumcised' (Gal. 2.7–9). And just in case you were wondering, the following ancient text kindly explains how to undo circumcision in what can be read on its own as one of the most spectacular examples of understatement:

> And, if the glans is bare and the man wishes for the look of the thing to have it covered, that can be done; but more easily in a boy than in a man; in one in whom the defect is natural, than in one in whom after the custom of certain races has been circumcised . . . Now the treatment for those in whom the defect is natural is as follows . . . . But in one who has been circumcised the prepuce is to be raised from the underlying penis around the circumference of the glans by means of a scalpel. This is not so very painful, for once the margin has been freed it can be stripped up by hand as far back as the pubes, nor in so doing is there any bleeding. The prepuce thus freed is again stretched forwards beyond the glans; next cold water affusions are freely used, and a plaster is applied . . . And for the following days the patient is to fast until nearly overcome by hunger lest satiety excite that part. (Celsus 7.25.1)[11]

FOOD AND DIFFERENCE

Though not quite as dramatic as circumcision, food laws were one of the ways in which Jews would differentiate themselves from Gentiles and how various people would differentiate themselves from Jews and mark Jews out as Jews in the ancient world. Biblical Law (Lev. 11; Deut. 14) mentions a variety of animals which may not be eaten by the people of Israel and, most famously, these were to include pig and shellfish. As with circumcision, the Maccabean crisis brought this legal issue to the fore and one story remembered in 2 Maccabees has one prominent Jew called Eleazar avoiding even pork-substitute. The passage is worth quoting in some detail:

> Eleazar, one of the scribes in high position, a man now advanced in age and of noble presence, was being forced to open his mouth to eat swine's flesh. But he, welcoming death with honour rather

than life with pollution, went up to the rack of his own accord, spitting out the flesh, as all ought to do who have the courage to refuse things that it is not right to taste, even for the natural love of life. Those who were in charge of that unlawful sacrifice took the man aside because of their long acquaintance with him, and privately urged him to bring meat of his own providing, proper for him to use, and pretend that he was eating the flesh of the sacrificial meal that had been commanded by the king, so that by doing this he might be saved from death . . . But making a high resolve, worthy of his years and the dignity of his old age and the grey hairs that he had reached with distinction and his excellent life even from childhood, and moreover according to holy God-given law, he declared himself quickly, telling them to send him to Hades.

'Such pretence is not worthy of our time of life', he said, 'for many of the young might suppose that Eleazar in his ninetieth year had gone over to an alien religion, and through my pretence, for the sake of living a brief moment longer, they would be led astray because of me, while I defile and disgrace my old age . . . Therefore, by bravely giving up my life now, I will show myself worthy of my old age and leave to the young a noble example of how to die a good death willingly and nobly for the revered and holy laws'. (2 Macc. 6.18–28)

Avoidance of pork, in particular, became one area of puzzlement for Gentiles. When the Jewish philosopher Philo recalled an audience with the Roman Emperor, Gaius Caligula, we find a clear example of such puzzlement in Caligula's questioning:

. . . he then asked a very important and solemn question; 'why is it that you abstain from eating pig's flesh?' And then again at this question such a violent laughter was raised by our adversaries, partly because they were really delighted, and partly as they wished to court the emperor out of flattery . . . (*Legat.* 361)

The Roman satirist, Juvenal, effectively claimed that Jews 'see no difference between eating swine's flesh, from which their father abstained, and that of man' (Juvenal, *Satires* 14.96). There are plenty of general (and slightly confused) comments by non-Jewish authors in the ancient world on the ways in which Jews would not eat with non-Jews. The following from the historian Tacitus is fairly typical: 'Jews are kind to one another but hostile to everyone else. They also eat separately' (Tacitus, introduction to *Histories* V). Notably, in Acts 10–11.18 it is the removal of the need to observe the food laws which is absolutely crucial in the spread of the movement in Jesus' name to include Gentiles as well as Jews.

It should probably come as no surprise, then, that the role of food is crucial in the portrayal, at least, of interaction or non-interaction between Jews and non-Jews. In general terms, the book of Tobit highlights the difference centred on food: 'After I was carried away captive to Assyria and came as a captive to Nineveh, everyone of my kindred and my people ate the food of the Gentiles, but I kept myself from eating the food of the Gentiles' (Tob. 1.10–11). Notice that the issue is not eating with Gentiles because they are Gentiles but the problem is emphatically the food of the Gentiles. In other words, from this perspective, why should a Jew eat, say, pork? In the book of Daniel there is a story (Dan. 1.3–17) of how Daniel and his companions would not eat the royal rations and would not drink wine and so they instead ate 'vegetables' (literally: 'seeds') so again food is the issue in some way, though whether this involved avoiding food such as pork or food dedicated to idols (or indeed both) is not entirely clear.

A more precise example of food seeming to be the barrier for Jewish-Gentile interaction, where idolatry certainly comes to the fore, is found in text called *Joseph and Aseneth*. The text is based on a simple problem for the writer which is found in Genesis: 'Pharaoh gave Joseph the name Zaphenath-paneah; and he gave him Asenath daughter of Potiphera, priest of On, as his wife. Thus Joseph gained authority over the land of Egypt' (Gen. 41.45). Does not this imply that Joseph was a little too close to idolatry for comfort? According to *Joseph and Aseneth*, the answer is an emphatic 'no':

> Joseph said . . . 'It is not right for a man who worships God, who with his mouth blesses the living God, and eats the blessed bread of life, and drinks the blessed cup of immortality . . . to kiss a strange woman, who with her mouth blesses dead and dumb idols, and eats of their table the bread of strangulation, and drinks of their libations the cup of treachery . . . it is not right for a woman who worships God to kiss a strange man, because this is an abomination in God's eyes . . .' (*Joseph and Aseneth* 8.5–8)

Quite what 'the bread of strangulation' might be is not clear but it is clear that idolatry plays a role in the differentiation between Jew and Gentile in this passage. The context of food and idolatry is further evident in the word 'abomination' (*bdelugma*) because it is associated not only with banned food in the Hebrew Bible/Old Testament but also frequently associated with fierce denunciations of idolatry. Once again we see reasons given for non-association with Gentiles: food and idolatry.

According to Acts, a blanket explanation for Jews not associating and not eating with Gentiles is given by Peter: 'You yourselves know that it is unlawful for a Jew to associate with or to visit a Gentile' (Acts 10.28). This is shortly followed up in Acts with related comments aimed at Peter in Jerusalem: 'So when Peter went up to Jerusalem, the circumcised believers criticized him, saying, "Why did you go to uncircumcised men and eat with them?" (Acts 11.2–3). There are similar sentiments found in early Judaism but once we look at such texts, fierce as some of them may be, the more specific reasons relating to idolatry and food, and not simply because Gentiles are Gentile, remain evident. A sectarian example comes from the book of *Jubilees*:

> Keep yourself separate from the nations, and do not eat with them; and do not imitate their rites, nor associate with them; for their rites are unclean and their practices polluted, an abomination and

unclean. They offer sacrifices to the dead and worship demons and they eat among the graves; yet all their rites are worthless and to no purpose. (*Jubilees* 22.16–17; cf. *t. 'Abod. Zar.* 4.6)

There were, however, differing views on Jewish association with Gentiles and the seemingly 'strict' views seem to be in the minority. 'Idolatrous' images were common enough and when Jews were present in baths or a theatre then it was possible to rationalize this by simply not giving the images any theological credence (m. *AZ* 3.4). Of course, on the ground there would have been all sorts of interaction between Jews and different non-Jewish groups, with various levels of assimilation, as John Barclay has shown in detail. Philip Harland has also shown how Jews, like other groups in ancient city life, had dual or multiple affiliations to different groups, from the synagogue to trade associations and thus providing a range of contacts and social interactions.[12]

The issue of food occurs regularly in discussions of Jews eating with Gentiles, as we have already seen, but this was hardly insurmountable. If the circumstances were right, if things like idolatry were avoided and food banned in the Torah removed from the meal table, then there is no reason in the abstract why Jews could not eat with non-Jews. In the early Jewish fiction, Judith, the heroine was a master of both undermining the enemy and avoiding of over-assimilation in the process:

So Holofernes said to her [Judith], 'Have a drink and be merry with us!' Judith said, 'I will gladly drink, my lord, because today is the greatest day in my whole life.' Then she took what her maid had prepared and ate and drank before him. Holofernes was greatly pleased with her, and drank a great quantity of wine, much more than he had ever drunk in any one day since he was born. (Jdt. 12.17–19)

Note here that it is made absolutely explicit that Judith the Jew ate food already prepared for her and, despite the unusual circumstances, this shows how table fellowship could be made possible by having food readily available in a not dissimilar way to observant Jews today having kosher meals on aeroplanes, for instance. It seems as if similar assumptions were read into the book of Esther. Esther was present at a (Gentile) banquet and so steps were made to make it clear that Esther was not behaving out of place. One Greek re-reading of the text says, 'And your servant has not eaten at Haman's table, and I have not honoured the king's feast or drunk the wine of libations' (Additions to Esther C 14.17). Notice here that the great worry is about the avoidance of idolatry. In everyday situations, an alternative solution to dealing with the problem of idolatrous food may simply to have been to avoid asking about the origin of the meat, perhaps following the logic of Paul:

> If an unbeliever invites you to a meal and you are disposed to go, eat whatever is set before you without raising any question on the ground of conscience. But if someone says to you, 'This has been offered in sacrifice', then do not eat it, out of consideration for the one who informed you, and for the sake of conscience – I mean the other's conscience, not your own. For why should my liberty be subject to the judgment of someone else's conscience? (1 Cor. 10.27–29)[13]

Probably the sweetest example of interaction between Jews and Gentiles at the meal table comes from the early Jewish text, the *Letter of Aristeas*:

> 'Everything of which you partake', he [the Egyptian king] said, 'will be served in compliance with your habits; it will be served to me as well as to you.' They expressed their pleasure and the king ordered the finest apartments to be given to them near the citadel, and the preparations for the banquet were made. (*Letter of Aristeas* 181)

It looks as if a not dissimilar kind of reasoning, though presumably less cordial, was happening among the first Christians in Rome:

Some believe in eating anything, while the weak eat only vegetables. Those who eat must not despise those who abstain, and those who abstain must not pass judgment on those who eat . . . Do not, for the sake of food, destroy the work of God. Everything is indeed clean, but it is wrong for you to make others fall by what you eat; it is good not to eat meat or drink wine or do anything that makes your brother or sister stumble. (Rom. 14.2–3, 20–21)

One obvious interpretation of this passage is that those eating vegetables were observing the food laws and were certain of doing so by staying effectively vegetarian, a phenomenon paralleled in the contemporary world in some contexts where observant Jews eat with non-Jews. The avoidance of wine could possibly be linked with Jewish avoidance of Gentile wine which we know from other sources, even if it is not entirely clear precisely why it was avoided. In general terms, Jewish avoidance of Gentile wine seems to have been linked with idolatry, again an issue at the heart of table fellowship between Jews and non-Jews. The avoidance of Gentile wine on the assumption that it is idolatrous appears to be assumed in the following example:

These things belonging to gentiles are prohibited, and the prohibition affecting them extends to deriving any benefit from them at all: wine, vinegar of gentiles which to begin with was wine . . . 'Meat which is being brought into an idol is permitted. But that which comes out is prohibited, because it is *like sacrifices of the dead* (Ps. 106.28)', the words of R. Aqiba. Those who are going to an idolatrous pilgrimage – it is prohibited to do business with them. (*m. 'Abod. Zar.* 2.3)

THE PROBLEM(S) WITH GENTILES

A common scholarly view, and one which is still found in scholarly literature, was that Gentiles had a special kind of impurity and therefore ought to be avoided in the same way impurity ought to be avoided.[14] The following was a key text:

> A proselyte who converted on the eve of Passover [the fourteenth of Nisan] – the House of Shammai say, 'He immerses himself and eats his Passover offering in the evening'. The House of Hillel say, 'He who takes his leave of the foreskin is as if he took his leave of the grave [and must be sprinkled on the third and seventh day after circumcision as if he had suffered corpse uncleanness'. (*m. Pesah.* 8.8)

Critics, however, have challenged the view of intrinsic Gentile impurity and pointed out that Gentiles can be *described* in the language of impurity in the sense of a simile, as if Gentiles were (say) impure like a menstruating woman. Jonathan Klawans and Christine E. Hayes have overthrown the scholarly idea that there was some kind of legal category of an intrinsic Gentile impurity. As Hayes shows, two crucial pieces of rabbinic evidence show just how problematic the idea of an intrinsic Gentile impurity is. According to the following passage, Gentiles are allowed to handle priestly food ('heave offering'): 'A gentile and a Samaritan – that which they separate is [valid] heave offering, and that which they take as tithes is [valid] tithes, and that which they dedicate [to the Temple] is [validly] dedicated' (*m. Ter.* 3.9). If Gentiles had intrinsic impurity then they would not be allowed the handle priestly food because it needs to be kept pure (see Chapter 3). For these reasons Gentiles should not be able to offer sacrifices if they were intrinsically impure yet they are clearly allowed to do so, as the following examples simply assume:[15]

> Said R. Simeon, 'Seven rules did the court ordain . . . (2) A gentile who sent his burnt offering from overseas and sent drink offerings with it – they are offered from what he has sent' (*m. Sheq.* 7.6)

> These are [meal offerings which] require oil and frankincense: . . . the meal offerings of gentiles . . . (*m. Men.* 5.3)

It is also notable that, as we have seen, in texts where Jewish and Gentile social interaction is discussed there is no concern for issues of impurity (cf. *m. Ber.* 7.1; *m. AZ* 5.5; and contrast rabbinic discussions of the 'people of the land' – see Chapter 3).

Instead, as Klawans and Hayes argue, it seems that the 'problem' with Gentiles was they were deemed to be mired in idolatry and *morally* impure. Intermarriage would therefore lead the righteous astray. This is grounded in several biblical texts such as the following not-so-subtle examples:

Thus the land became defiled; and I punished it for its iniquity, and the land vomited out its inhabitants. But you shall keep my statutes and my ordinances and commit none of these abominations, either the citizen or the alien who resides among you (for the inhabitants of the land, who were before you, committed all of these abominations, and the land became defiled) . . . (Lev. 18.25–27)

When the Lord your God brings you into the land that you are about to enter and occupy, and he clears away many nations before you – the Hittites, the Girgashites, the Amorites, the Canaanites, the Perizzites, the Hivites, and the Jebusites, seven nations mightier and more numerous than you – and when the Lord your God gives them over to you and you defeat them, then you must utterly destroy them. Make no covenant with them and show them no mercy. Do not intermarry with them, giving your daughters to their sons or taking their daughters for your sons, for that would turn away your children from following me, to serve other gods. Then the anger of the Lord would be kindled against you, and he would destroy you quickly. (Deut. 7.1–4; cf. Lev. 18.26; 1 Kgs 11.1–2; Ezra 9.1–3, 10–12; Neh. 13.26)

These sorts of sentiment were taken up in early Jewish texts. From the Dead Sea Scrolls we get the following: 'When he saw that the peoples of [the ea]rth behaved abominably . . . all the earth [became] impure defilement altogether' (4Q381 frag. 69, 1–2; see also *Jub.* 22.16–20, discussed above). In addition to idolatry, Gentiles were liable to perform acts such as murder and sexual immorality. Again, this was grounded in biblical texts and developed in early Jewish texts (cf. Exod. 34.15–16; Lev. 18.24–30; Deut. 7.2–4, 16; 20.18; *Jub.* 9.15; *Aristeas* 152; Philo, *Spec. Laws* 1.51; *Sib. Or.* 3.492, 496–500; 5.168; Tob. 14.6).

In addition to food, but in some ways related to food, what we might call morality was another feature of Jewish-Gentile interaction. One way the concern for Gentile behaviour would manifest itself was in 'vice-lists' such as the following example from a the first century Jewish text, Wisdom of Solomon, as a record of the sorts of things idolaters do:

> . . . and all is a raging riot of blood and murder, theft and deceit, corruption, faithlessness, tumult, perjury, confusion over what is good, forgetfulness of favours, defiling of souls, sexual perversion, disorder in marriages, adultery, and debauchery. (Wis. 14.25–26)

Just as food issues found their way into early Christian dealings with Gentiles, so did vice-lists and concern for Gentile behaviour. Paul used vice lists when, for instance, describing the past lives of the Corinthian Christians and a warning to their present and future (1 Cor. 6.9–11) while 1 Peter explicitly makes reference to what is deemed stereotypical Gentile behaviour:

> You have already spent enough time in doing what the Gentiles like to do, living in licentiousness, passions, drunkenness, revels, carousing, and lawless idolatry. They are surprised that you no longer join them in the same excesses of dissipation and so they blaspheme you . . . (1 Pet. 4.3–5)

One possible way of interaction between Jews and Gentiles, particularly for Jews less convinced about Gentile behaviour, was through the so-called Noachide laws, given, of course, to humanity and before the commandments at Sinai were given more specifically to the Israelites. These laws were based on Gen. 9.3–6:

Every moving thing that lives shall be food for you; and just as I gave you the green plants, I give you everything. Only, you shall not eat flesh with its life, that is, its blood. For your own lifeblood I will surely require a reckoning: from every animal I will require it and from human beings, each one for the blood of another, I will require a reckoning for human life. Whoever sheds the blood of a human, by a human shall that person's blood be shed; for in his own image God made humankind.

A key rabbinic passage relating to the Noachide laws is from the Tosefta: 'Seven commandments were given to the children of Noah: regarding the establishments of courts of justice, idolatry, blasphemy, fornication, bloodshed, theft [and the torn limb]' (t. 'Abodah Zarah 8.4). Later still, three Noachide concerns involve capital offences, namely, fornication, bloodshed and blasphemy or idolatry, and then become the minimum test case for allegiance to Judaism for Jews (b. Sanh. 57a, 74a) and so we may be dealing with something like a universal code for Jews and Gentiles.[16] Related concerns were certainly found by the time of the writing of the New Testament texts. According to *Jubilees*,

. . . in the twenty-eighth jubilee Noah began to command his grandsons with ordinances and commandments and all of the judgments which he knew. And he bore witness to his sons so that they might do justice and cover the shame of their flesh and bless the one who created them and honour father and mother, and each one love his neighbour and preserve themselves from fornication and pollution and from all injustice . . . And everyone sold himself in order that he might do injustice and pour out much blood, and the earth was full of much injustice . . . And they poured out much blood upon the earth . . . For all who eat the blood of man and all who eat the blood of any flesh will be blotted out, all of them . . . And you shall not eat living flesh lest it be that your blood which is your life be sought by the hand of all flesh which eats upon the earth . . . (*Jub.* 7.20, 23–24, 28–33)

In Acts 15, something similar to the Noachide laws is used to deal with the issue of Gentiles in the earliest Christian movement. The conclusion is that Gentiles 'turning to God' should be written to with the following instructions: 'abstain only from things polluted by idols and from fornication/*porneia* and from whatever has been strangled and from blood' (Acts 15.20; cf. 15.29). Related concerns also come through several times in the book of Revelation (e.g. Rev. 2.14; 9.20–21), a book deeply concerned about interactions with the Roman world. For instance, there is polemic aimed at those who 'tolerate that woman Jezebel, who calls herself a prophet and is teaching and beguiling my servants to practice fornication and to eat food sacrificed to idols' (2.20) and where there is a brutal end for those who do not adhere to laws clearly reminiscent of the Noachide laws: 'as for the cowardly, the faithless, the polluted, the murderers, the fornicators, the sorcerers, the idolaters and all liars, their place will be in the lake that burns with fire and sulphur, which is the second death' (Rev. 21.8).

SUMMARY

Views of family were important for some Jews in establishing who was a Jew: having Jewish parents made it easier to identify as a Jew with minimal controversy. New Testament scholars have rightly pointed out that family and respect for parents can be very important but too often at the expense of overlooking the prioritizing of family. For instance, some people felt that commandments were more important than family and we should not forget that at the time and in the place of Jesus there were notable social upheavals whereby traditional family models and roles were turned upside down. In terms of marking who was a male Jew, circumcision was obviously important and doubly so since it became a symbol of Jewish loyalty in the Maccabean crisis. However, circumcision also becomes the final hurdle for conversion to Judaism (for men) and this was not always attractive for interested Gentiles. This led to some debates over what it took to become a 'Jew'. It is no surprise that circumcision becomes a flashpoint as the message spreads among Gentiles. Food and eating habits were also ways in which Jewish identity was perceived and constructed and, again, issues such as the avoidance of pork could function as a symbol of Jewish loyalty in light of the Maccabean crisis. Contrary to some scholarly views, Jews were able to eat with Gentiles. In the texts available it seems that, if the problems of idolatry and food banned in biblical law could be avoided by Jews, then there should be no problem with Jewish-Gentile interaction. Not everyone accepted this, at least not without significant qualification. A more sectarian view involved still avoiding Gentiles at all costs. Gentiles were, according to some stereotypical views, liable to be involved in all sorts of immoral acts, from idolatry to murder. Indeed, such 'moral' issues were an issue, at least in the texts we have, in issues of intermarriage. Some Jews also developed a series of basis laws which would further allow basic Jewish-Gentile interaction. Unsurprisingly, all the above issues come through in those New Testament texts where Jewish-Gentile interaction is a crucial issue.

CONCLUDING REMARKS

We have seen, then, plenty of Jewish texts relating to legal, or quasi-legal, issues in early Judaism. It ought to be clear by now that there was a great deal of diversity and (sometimes violent) debate over what was, for some, the source of Jewish identity in the ancient world, the Torah. There is still much work to do on the detailed application of Jewish legal texts to New Testament passages. In terms of historical Jesus studies, the idea of Jesus and the Law continues to be full of arguments whereby Jesus still has to override at least one commandment in some way. This may be the case historically, but given the range of legal views in early Judaism it should at least be done after an exhaustive study of parallels in Jewish legal texts. That said, some recent work is now showing that Jesus' views on the Law were all paralleled in early Judaism.[1]

The appreciation of Jewish Law and legal texts still needs much more work in the study of Christian origins in general, not least because Christian identity would regularly manifest itself over against practice of the Torah. In the scholarly study of Christian origins there are still numerous caricatures of Jewish Law but I just want to give the final example of recent developments in continental philosophy where Paul has become an important intellectual figure. Following Jacob Taubes' lead, famous contemporary thinkers such as Alain Badiou and Slavoj Žižek have seen Paul as an important revolutionary and universalist thinker, a kind of proto-Marxist.[2] Jewish Law is an important feature in this debate and some scholars are worried that the old model of a negative Judaism is being continued without aware-ness of the history of New Testament scholarship. It must be stressed, however, that Badiou and others certainly seem to be on to something in certain cases. According to Badiou, Paul would not compromise when it came to fidelity to his revolutionary principles of the new movement. As for the Law, Badiou adds, Paul is not opposed to it as such but he is indifferent ('Circumcision is nothing, and uncircumci-sion is nothing' – 1 Cor. 7.19), though Badiou believes that indifference is worse. This is because the new universality, unlike the Torah, bears no privileged relation to the Jewish community.[3] This, as we saw in Chapter 5, does echo Paul's view of food laws in Romans.

However, there is some evidence that old negative views concern-ing Jewish Law are difficult to leave behind. Terry Eagleton, whose work we have seen in passing in this book, is both a fan of Badiou's work on Paul and recent defender of Christianity and 'religion' against its critics, makes uncomfortable claims concerning the Law:

It is this overturning of the Satanic or super-egoic image of God in Jesus that offers to unlock the lethal deadlock between Law and desire, or what Jacques Lacan calls the Real. It is a condition in which we come to fall morbidly in love with the Law itself, and with the oppressed, unhappy state to which it reduces us, desiring nothing more than to punish ourselves for our guilt even unto death. This is why Saint Paul describes the Law as cursed. It is this urge to do away with ourselves as so much waste and garbage to which Freud gives the name of the death drive, the opposite of which is an unconditionally accepting love. As Paul writes, the Law, and the sin or guilt which it generates, is what brings death into the world. The choice is between a life liberated from this pathological deadlock, which is known to the Gospel as eternal life, and that grisly caricature of eternal life which is the ghastly pseudo-immortality of the death drive. It is a state in which we prevent ourselves from dying for real by clinging desperately to our morbid pleasure in death as a way of affirming that we are alive . . . This is the hell . . . of those who are stuck fast in their masochistic delight in the Law, and spit in the face of those who offer to relieve them of this torture . . . To be unburdened of their guilt is to be deprived of the very sickness which keeps them going. This, one might claim, is the primary masochism known as religion.[4]

Given the details of the Law given in this book, from Sabbath observance to circumcision, has not this quotation from Eagleton got some highly unfair implications? Aren't such views concerning Jewish Law worth testing with direct reference to Jewish Law . . .?

NOTES

INTRODUCTION

[1] I have analysed the historical and cultural reasons underlying the shifts in scholarly rhetoric concerning the role of Jewish Law in J. G. Crossley, *Jesus in an Age of Terror: Scholarly Projects for a New American Century* (London and Oakville: Equinox, 2008), Chapters 5–6.

[2] N. T. Wright, *Jesus and the Victory of God* (London: SPCK, 1996), pp. 399–402.

CHAPTER 1

[1] Indeed, for full discussion of what follows see H. G. M. Williamson, *Ezra, Nehemiah: Word Biblical Commentary 16* (Waco: Word, 1985).

[2] E.g. J. Neusner, *Rabbinic Traditions about the Pharisees before 70* (3 vols; Leiden: Brill, 1971); D. Instone-Brewer, *Traditions of the Rabbis from the Era of the New Testament, vol. 1 Prayer and Agriculture* (Grand Rapids: Eerdmans, 2004).

[3] M. Hengel and R. Deines, 'E. P. Sanders' "Common Judaism", Jesus, and the Pharisees', *JTS* 46 (1995), pp. 1–70.

[4] E. P. Sanders, *Jewish Law from Jesus to the Mishnah: Five Studies* (London: SCM, 1990), p. 273.

[5] J. M. G. Barclay, *Jews in the Mediterranean Diaspora from Alexander to Trajan (323 BCE–117 CE)* (Edinburgh: T&T Clark, 1996).

[6] M. Casey, *From Jewish Prophet to Gentile God: The Origins and Development of New Testament Christology* (Louisville: Westminster John Knox; Cambridge: James Clarke, 1991), p. 19.

[7] See further J. G. Crossley, 'The Damned Rich (Mk 10.17–31)', *ExpT* 116 (2005), pp. 397–401; J. G. Crossley, *Why Christianity Happened: A Socio-historical Explanation of Christian Origins 26–50 CE* (Louisville: WJK, 2006), Chapter 2.

[8] See further e.g. R. J. Bauckham, 'Rich Man and Lazarus: The Parable and the Parallels', *NTS* 37 (1991), pp. 225–46.

NOTES

CHAPTER 2

[1] T. Eagleton, *Reason, Faith, and Revolution: Reflections on the God Debate* (New Haven and London: Yale University Press. 2009), pp. 10–11.
[2] A. Cowley (ed.), *Aramaic Papyri of the Fifth Century B.C.* (Oxford: Clarendon, 1923).
[3] E. P. Sanders, *Jewish Law from Jesus to the Mishnah: Five Studies* (London: SCM, 1990), p. 20.
[4] M. Casey, *Aramaic Sources of Mark's Gospel* (Cambridge: CUP, 1998), pp. 173–92.

CHAPTER 3

[1] See J. Neusner, *The Idea of Purity in Ancient Judaism* (Leiden: Brill, 1973).
[2] It is perhaps worth citing a lengthier bibliography than normal given the highly controversial nature of the debate over purity. For a selection see e.g. J. Neusner, *Rabbinic Traditions about the Pharisees before 70* (3 vols; Leiden: Brill, 1971); E. P. Sanders, *Jewish Law From the Bible to the Mishnah* (London: SCM, 1990), pp. 131–254; J. D. G. Dunn, *Jesus Paul and the Law: Studies in Mark and Galatians* (London: SPCK, 1990), pp. 61–88; H. K. Harrington, 'Did Pharisees Eat Ordinary Food in a State of Ritual Purity?', *JSJ* 26 (1995), pp. 42–54; B. Chilton, 'E. P. Sanders and the Question of Purity', in B. Chilton and C. A. Evans (eds), *Jesus in Context: Temple, Purity, and Restoration* (Leiden: Brill, 1997), pp. 221–30; E. Regev, 'Pure Individualism: The Idea of Non-Priestly Purity in Ancient Judaism', *JSJ* 31(2000), pp. 176–202; J. C. Poirier, 'Purity beyond the Temple in the Second Temple Era', *JBL* 122 (2003), pp. 247–65.
[3] See further R. P. Booth, *Jesus and the Laws of Purity: Tradition and Legal History in Mark 7* (Sheffield: JSOT Press, 1986); J. G. Crossley, *The Date of Mark's Gospel: Insights from the Law in Earliest Christianity* (London and New York: T&T Clark/Continuum, 2004), Chapter 7.
[4] J. C. Poirier, 'Why did the Pharisees Wash their Hands?', *JJS* 47 (1996), pp. 217–33.
[5] J. G. Crossley, 'Halakah and Mark 7.4: " . . and beds"', *JSNT* 25 (2003), pp. 433–47.
[6] For a full discussion with bibliography see J. G. Crossley, *Why Christianity Happened: A Sociohistorical Account of Christian Origins 26–50 CE* (Louisville: WJK, 2006), Chapter 4.

CHAPTER 4

[1] For more on the issue of adultery and punishment in Jewish Law see D. Instone-Brewer, *Divorce and Remarriage in the Bible: The Social and Literary Context* (Grand Rapids: Eerdmans, 2002).
[2] M. Bockmuehl, *Jewish Law in the Gentile Churches: Halakah and the Beginning of Christian Public Ethics* (T&T Clark: Edinburgh, 2000), pp. 17–21.
[3] Instone-Brewer, *Divorce and Remarriage in the Bible*, pp. 145–6.

NOTES

4   See T. Holmén, 'Divorce in CD 4.20–5.2 and in 11Q 57.17–18: Some Remarks
on the Pertinence of the Question', *RevQ* 18 (1998), pp. 397–408; D. Instone-
Brewer, 'Nomological Exegesis in Qumran "Divorce Texts', *RevQ* 18 (1998),
pp. 561–79.

5   A. Cowley (ed.), *Aramaic Papyri of the Fifth Century B.C.* (Oxford: Clarendon,
1923), pp. 44–50, Papyrus 15, line 23.

6   D. Instone-Brewer, 'Jewish Women Divorcing Their Husbands in Early Judaism:
The Background to Papyrus Se'elim 13', *HTR* 92 (1999), pp. 349–57. For
different interpretations see T. Ilan, 'Notes and Observations on a Newly
Published Divorce Bill from the Judean Desert', *HTR* 89 (1996), pp. 195–202;
A. Schremer, 'Divorce in Papyrus Se'elim 13 Once Again: A Reply to Tal Ilan',
HTR 91 (1998), pp. 193–202. For the text see A. Yardeni, in H. M. Cotton and
A. Yardeni (eds), *Discoveries in the Judean Desert XXVII. Aramaic, Hebrew
and Greek Documentary Texts from Nahal Hever and Other Sites* (Oxford:
Clarendon, 1997), pp. 65–70.

7   Sanders, *Jewish Law*, pp. 51–2.

8   G. Vermes, *The Religion of Jesus the Jew* (London: SCM, 1993), pp. 35–36.

CHAPTER 5

1   On the controversial debates over the historical usefulness of the term 'Jew'
see e.g. B. J. Malina and R. L. Rohrbaugh, *Social-Science Commentary on the
Gospel of John* (Minneapolis: Fortress Press, 1998), pp. 44–45; J. H. Elliott,
'Jesus the Israelite was Neither a "Jew" nor a "Christian": On Correcting
Misleading Nomenclature', *JSHJ* 5 (2007), pp. 119–54; P. F. Esler, *Conflict
and Identity in Romans: The Social Setting of Paul's Letter* (Minneapolis:
Fortress, 2003); S. Mason, 'Jews, Judeans, Judaizing, Judaism: Problems of
Categorization in Ancient History', *JSJ* 38 (2007), pp. 457–512. For ideolo-
gical questions raised see A. J. Levine, *The Misunderstood Jew: The Church
and the Scandal of the Jewish Jesus* (San Francisco: HarperCollins, 2006);
J. G. Crossley, 'Jesus the Jew since 1967', in H. Moxnes, W. Blanton, and
J. G. Crossley (eds), *Jesus beyond Nationalism: Constructing the Historical
Jesus in a Period of Cultural Complexity* (London and Oakville: Equinox,
2009), pp. 111–29.

2   S. J. D. Cohen, *The Beginnings of Jewishness: Boundaries, Varieties, Uncer-
tainties* (Berkeley, Los Angeles and London: University of California Press,
1999), pp. 263–307. On the tricky question of Timothy's 'Jewishness' and his
parents see pp. 363–77.

3   See further, M. Bockmuehl, 'Let the Dead Bury their Dead (Mt. 8.22/
Lk. 9.60): Jesus and the Halakah', *JTS* 49 (1998), pp. 553–81.

4   See further S. C. Barton, *Discipleship and Family Ties in Mark and Matthew*
(Cambridge: CUP, 1995).

5   T. W. Manson, *The Sayings of Jesus* (London: SCM, 1957), p. 131; Barton,
Family, pp. 169–70.

6   Bockmuehl, 'Let the Dead Bury their Dead'; M. Bockmuehl, 'Leave the
Dead to Bury their own Dead: A Brief Clarification in Reply to Crispin H. T.
Fletcher-Louis', *JSNT* 26 (2003), pp. 241–42.

[7] T. Eagleton, *Reason, Faith, and Revolution: Reflections on the God Debate* (New Haven and London: Yale University Press), p. 31.

[8] H. Moxnes, *Putting Jesus in His Place: A Radical Vision of Household and Kingdom* (Louisville: WJK, 2003), pp. 46–107.

[9] J. D. G. Dunn, *Jesus Paul and the Law: Studies in Mark and Galatians* (London: SPCK, 1990), pp. 129–182.

[10] Cf. Cohen, *Beginnings of Jewishness*, p. 227.

[11] L. L. Grabbe, *Judaism from Cyrus to Hadrian* (London: SCM, 1992).

[12] J. M. G. Barclay, *Jews in the Mediterranean Diaspora from Alexander to Trajan (323 BCE–117 CE)* (Edinburgh: T&T Clark, 1996); P. A. Harland, 'Social Networks and Connections with the Elites in the World of the Early Christians', in A. J. Blasi, P.-A. Turcotte and J. Duhaime (eds), *Handbook of Early Christianity and the Social Sciences* (Walnut Creek: AltaMira, 2002), pp. 385–408; P. A. Harland, *Associations, Synagogues, and Congregations: Claiming a Place in Ancient Mediterranean Society* (Minneapolis: Fortress, 2003), pp. 33–6, 177–264.

[13] See further Sanders, *Jewish Law*, pp. 272–83.

[14] The classic and most learned exposition of this view is G. Alon, 'The Levitical Uncleanness of Gentiles', in *Jews, Judaism and the Classical World: Studies in Jewish History in the Times of the Second Temple and Talmud* (Jerusalem: Magnes, 1977), pp. 146–89.

[15] C. E. Hayes, *Gentile Impurities and Jewish Identities: Intermarriage and Conversion from the Bible to the Talmud* (Oxford: OUP, 2002), pp. 107–44, 199–221.

[16] Bockmuehl, *Jewish Law*, pp. 145–73, esp. 161.

CONCLUDING REMARKS

[1] Cf. e.g. G. Vermes, *The Religion of Jesus the Jew* (London: SCM, 1993); J. G. Crossley, *The Date of Mark's Gospel: Insights from the Law in Earliest Christianity* (London & New York: T&T Clark/Continuum, 2004), Chapters 4, 6 and 7; D. Catchpole, *Jesus People: The Historical Jesus and the Beginnings of Community* (London: Darton, Longman and Todd; Grand Rapids: Baker, 2006); M. Casey, *Jesus of Nazareth: An Independent Historian's Account of his Life and Teachings* (London and New York: T&T Clark/Continuum, 2010).

[2] E.g. J. Taubes, *The Political Theology of Paul* (Stanford: Stanford University Press, 2004); A. Badiou, *Saint Paul: The Foundation of Universalism* (Stanford: California, 2003); S. Žižek, *The Puppet and the Dwarf: The Perverse Core of Christianity* (Cambridge, Mass.: MIT Press, 2003).

[3] Badiou, *Saint Paul*, p. 23.

[4] T. Eagleton, *Reason, Faith, and Revolution: Reflections on the God Debate* (New Haven and London: Yale University Press, 2009), pp. 21–22.

BIBLIOGRAPHY

USEFUL PRIMARY SOURCES

Aberbach, M. and Grossfeld, B. (eds), *Targum Onkelos to Genesis* (New York: Ktav, 1982).

Charlesworth, J. H. (ed.), *The Old Testament Pseudepigrapha* (2 vols; New York: Doubleday, 1983–85).

Clarke, E. G. (ed.), *Targum Pseudo-Jonathan of the Pentateuch* (Hoboken: Ktav, 1984).

Colson, F. H., et al. (eds), Philo's *Works* (12 vols; London: Heinemann, 1929–53).

Cowley, A. (ed.), *Aramaic Papyri of the Fifth Century BC* (Oxford: Clarendon Press, 1923).

Danby, H. (ed.), *The Mishnah* (Oxford: Oxford University Press, 1933).

Drazin, I. (ed.), *Targum Onkelos to Deuteronomy* (New York: Ktav, 1981).

—(ed.), *Targum Onkelos to Exodus* (Denver: Ktav, 1990).

—(ed.), *Targum Onkelos to Leviticus* (Denver: Ktav, 1994).

Epstein, I. (ed.), *The Hebrew–English Edition of the Babylonian Talmud* (36 vols; London: Soncino, 1960–90).

Grossfeld, B. (ed.), *The Targum Onqelos to Leviticus and the Targum Onqelos to Numbers* (Edinburgh: T&T Clark, 1988).

Lauterbach, J. Z. (ed.), *Mekilta de-Rabbi Ishmael* (3 vols; Philadelphia: Jewish Publication Society of America, 1949).

Martínez, F. G. and Tigchelaar, E. J. C. (eds), *The Dead Sea Scrolls Study Edition* (2 vols; Leiden: Brill, 1997–98).

Neusner, J., *The Mishnah: A New Translation* (Yale: Yale University Press, 1988).

—et al. (eds), *The Tosefta* (6 vols; New York: Ktav, 1977–86).

—et al. (eds), *The Talmud of the Land of Israel* (35 vols; Chicago: University of Chicago Press, 1982–94).

Stern, M. (ed.), *Greek and Latin Authors on Jews and Judaism* (3 vols; Jerusalem: Israel Academy of Sciences and Humanities, 1974).

Thackeray, H. St. J. et al. (eds), *Josephus' Works* (9 vols; London: Heinemann, 1929–53).

Vermes, G. (ed.), *The Complete Dead Sea Scrolls in English* (London: Penguin, 1997).

WORKS CITED

Alon, G., *Jews, Judaism and the Classical World: Studies in Jewish History in the Times of the Second Temple and Talmud* (Jerusalem: Magnes, 1977).

Badiou, A., *Saint Paul: The Foundation of Universalism* (Stanford: California, 2003).

Barclay, J. M. G., *Jews in the Mediterranean Diaspora from Alexander to Trajan (323 BCE–117 CE)* (Edinburgh: T&T Clark, 1996).

Bauckham, R. J., 'Rich Man and Lazarus: The Parable and the Parallels', *NTS* 37 (1991), pp. 225–46.

Bockmuehl, M., *Jewish Law in the Gentile Churches: Halakah and the Beginning of Christian Public Ethics* (T&T Clark: Edinburgh, 2000).

Booth, R. P., *Jesus and the Laws of Purity: Tradition and Legal History in Mark 7* (Sheffield: JSOT Press, 1986).

Casey, M., *From Jewish Prophet to Gentile God: The Origins and Development of New Testament Christology* (Louisville: Westminster John Knox; Cambridge: James Clarke, 1991).

—*Aramaic Sources of Mark's Gospel* (Cambridge: CUP, 1998).

—*Jesus of Nazareth: An Independent Historian's Account of his Life and Teachings* (London and New York: T&T Clark/Continuum, 2010).

Catchpole, D., *Jesus People: The Historical Jesus and the Beginnings of Community* (London: Darton, Longman and Todd; Grand Rapids: Baker, 2006).

Chilton, B., 'E. P. Sanders and the Question of Purity', in B. Chilton and C. A. Evans (eds), *Jesus in Context: Temple, Purity, and Restoration* (Leiden: Brill, 1997), pp. 221–30.

Crossley, J. G., 'Halakah and Mark 7.4: "... and beds"', *JSNT* 25 (2003), pp. 433–47.

—*The Date of Mark's Gospel: Insights from the Law in Earliest Christianity* (London and New York: T&T Clark/Continuum, 2004).

—'The Damned Rich (Mark 10.17–31)', *ExpT* 116 (2005), pp. 397–401.

—*Why Christianity Happened: A Sociohistorical Explanation of Christian Origins 26–50 CE* (Louisville: WJK, 2006).

—*Jesus in an Age of Terror: Scholarly Projects for a New American Century* (London and Oakville: Equinox, 2008).

—'Jesus the Jew since 1967', in H. Moxnes, W. Blanton and J. G. Crossley (eds), *Jesus beyond Nationalism: Constructing the Historical Jesus in a Period of Cultural Complexity* (London and Oakville: Equinox, 2009), pp. 111–29.

Dunn, J. D. G., *Jesus Paul and the Law: Studies in Mark and Galatians* (London: SPCK, 1990).

Eagleton, T., *Reason, Faith, and Revolution: Reflections on the God Debate* (New Haven and London: Yale University Press. 2009).

Elliott, J. H., 'Jesus the Israelite Was Neither a "Jew" nor a "Christian": On Correcting Misleading Nomenclature', *JSHJ* 5 (2007), pp. 119–54.

Esler, P. F., *Conflict and Identity in Romans: The Social Setting of Paul's Letter* (Minneapolis: Fortress, 2003).

Grabbe, L. L., *Judaism from Cyrus to Hadrian* (London: SCM, 1992).

Harland, P. A., 'Social Networks and Connections with the Elites in the World of the Early Christians', in A. J. Blasi, P.-A. Turcotte and J. Duhaime (eds),

Handbook of Early Christianity and the Social Sciences (Walnut Creek: AltaMira, 2002), pp. 385–408.

—*Associations, Synagogues, and Congregations: Claiming a Place in Ancient Mediterranean Society* (Minneapolis: Fortress, 2003).

Harrington, H. K., 'Did Pharisees Eat Ordinary Food in a State of Ritual Purity?', *JSJ* 26 (1995), pp. 42–54.

Hayes, C. E., *Gentile Impurities and Jewish Identities: Intermarriage and Conversion from the Bible to the Talmud* (Oxford: OUP, 2002).

Hengel, M. and Deines, R., 'E. P. Sanders' "Common Judaism", Jesus, and the Pharisees', *JTS* 46 (1995), pp. 1–70.

Holmén, T., 'Divorce in CD 4:20–5:2 and in 11Q 57.17–18: Some Remarks on the Pertinence of the Question', *RevQ* 18 (1998), pp. 397–408.

Ilan, T., 'Notes and Observations on a Newly Published Divorce Bill from the Judean Desert', *HTR* 89 (1996), pp. 195–202.

Instone–Brewer, D., 'Nomological Exegesis in Qumran "Divorce Texts', *RevQ* 18 (1998), pp. 561–79.

—'Jewish Women Divorcing Their Husbands in Early Judaism: The Background to Papyrus Se'elim 13', *HTR* 92 (1999), pp. 349–57.

—*Divorce and Remarriage in the Bible: The Social and Literary Context* (Grand Rapids: Eerdmans, 2002).

—*Traditions of the Rabbis from the Era of the New Testament, vol.1 Prayer and Agriculture* (Grand Rapids: Eerdmans, 2004).

Levine, A. J., *The Misunderstood Jew: The Church and the Scandal of the Jewish Jesus* (San Francisco: HarperCollins, 2006).

Malina, B. J., and Rohrbaugh, R. L., *Social–Science Commentary on the Gospel of John* (Minneapolis: Fortress Press, 1998).

Mason, S., 'Jews, Judeans, Judaizing, Judaism: Problems of Categorization in Ancient History', *JSJ* 38 (2007), pp. 457–512.

Neusner, J., *Rabbinic Traditions about the Pharisees before 70* (3 vols; Leiden: Brill, 1971).

—*The Idea of Purity in Ancient Judaism* (Leiden: Brill, 1973).

Poirier, J. C.,'Why did the Pharisees Wash their Hands?', *JJS* 47 (1996), pp. 217–33.

—'Purity beyond the Temple in the Second Temple Era', *JBL* 122 (2003), pp. 247–65.

Regev, E., 'Pure Individualism: The Idea of Non–Priestly Purity in Ancient Judaism', *JSJ* 31 (2000), pp. 176–202.

Sanders, E. P., *Jewish Law from Jesus to the Mishnah: Five Studies* (London: SCM, 1990).

Schremer, A., 'Divorce in Papyrus Se'elim 13 Once Again: A Reply to Tal Ilan', *HTR* 91 (1998), pp. 193–202.

Taubes, J., *The Political Theology of Paul* (Stanford: Stanford University Press, 2004).

Williamson, H. G. M., *Ezra, Nehemiah: Word Biblical Commentary 16* (Waco: Word, 1985).

Wright, N. T., *Jesus and the Victory of God* (London: SPCK, 1996).

Vermes, G., *The Religion of Jesus the Jew* (London: SCM, 1993).

Žižek, S., *The Puppet and the Dwarf: The Perverse Core of Christianity* (Cambridge, Mass.: MIT Press, 2003).

SOME (AND ONLY SOME) FURTHER GENERAL READING ON THE LAW AND THE NEW TESTAMENT

Allison, D. C., *Resurrecting Jesus: The Earliest Christian Tradition and Its Interpreters* (London: T&T Clark, 2005).

Banks, R., *Jesus and the Law in the Synoptic Tradition* (Cambridge: CUP, 1975).

Barton, S. C., *Discipleship and Family Ties in Mark and Matthew* (Cambridge: CUP, 1995).

Betz, H. D., *The Sermon on the Mount* (Minneapolis: Fortress, 1995).

Boyarin, D., *A Radical Jew: Paul and the Politics of Identity* (Berkeley and Los Angeles: University of California Press, 1994).

Holmén, T., *Jesus and Jewish Covenantal Thinking* (Leiden: Brill, 2001).

Jackson, B. S., *Essays on Halakhah in the New Testament* (Leiden: Brill, 2008).

Kazen, T., *Jesus and Purity Halakhah: Was Jesus Indifferent to Impurity?* (Stockholm : Almqvist & Wiksell International, 2002).

Loader, W. R. G., *Jesus' Attitude towards the Law* (Tübingen: Mohr Siebeck, 1997).

Meier, J. P., *A Marginal Jew: Rethinking the Historical Jesus. Law and Love* (New York: Doubleday, 2009).

Neusner, J., Chilton, B. D., and Levine, B. A., *Torah Revealed, Torah Fulfilled: Scriptural Laws in Formative Judaism and Earliest Christianity* (London and New York: T&T Clark/Continuum, 2008).

Sanders, E. P., *Paul and Palestinian Judaism: A Comparison of Patterns of Religion* (London: SCM, 1977).

—*Jesus and Judaism* (London: SCM, 1985).

Tomson, P. J., *Paul and the Jewish Law: Halakah in the Letters of the Apostle to the Gentiles* (Fortress Press: Minneapolis, 1990).

Westerholm, S., *Jesus and Scribal Authority*, (Lund: Gleerup, 1978).

INDEX